Find Your Wings and Fly

Dear Jo
Hope you enjoy
reading this!
All the best
Nushin

www.findyourwingsandfly.co.uk

FIND YOUR WINGS AND FLY

Life Lessons from the Cockpit

NUSHIN ELAHI

Published in 2022 by Reframe Press

Cover photograph: Burgh Island from the air, Devon.
© Nushin Elahi

Paperback ISBN: 978-1-7392495-0-2

Once you have tasted flight,

you will forever walk the earth with your eyes turned skyward,

for there you have been, and there you will always long to return.

— Leonardo da Vinci

This book is dedicated

to the memory of my mother, Alice Elahi, who showed me what an authentic life was,

to the men who helped me find my wings:

who first showed me the view of angels,

who always inspired me,

who made me captain of my plane,

who never lost sight of the joy, despite the challenge,

to my husband, without whose loving support none of this would have happened,

and

to all the many pilots out there, who continue to feel the magic.

Contents

Foreword

Hello, my name is Ted Barrett. At 98, I am the oldest practising pilot in the UK, and I have known Nushin since the first day she walked into the clubhouse at the airfield. Back then, she wasn't sure at all that she wanted to learn to fly herself. In fact, she kept insisting she didn't want that. I was always happy to encourage her to take up flying and get her licence. I knew she could do it. I know once you have tried it, it gets into your blood. It's why I still love to fly.

Nushin and I spent many hours sitting in the clubhouse talking. I would tell her about my life and what I had done. She would tell me about her mother, the art she loves, and her life. We really hit it off. There were times when she was in tears or clashing with the instructor. I would always tell her, 'Don't worry about the people, it's the flying that matters! It's no use comparing yourself to anybody else; you just do what you can.'

I was Nushin's first passenger, and I will always fly with her whenever she offers me a flight. I have absolute confidence in her as a pilot. She's a wonderful woman and a very good pilot. Very confident and capable. There's not much she can't do. She'll stick with it and get through.

Over the years we have become good friends. We've had some great times together. We once went up to an auction in Ely to sell some paintings, which was fun. She always takes me out for lunch on my birthday with other club members. We have also had some wonderful flights together, and every time her flying is superb. Once, when we flew back from Old Warden, the exhaust came loose. Even though I am an engine inspector, she heard it first. Another trip from Duxford was very turbulent, but she kept her cool. I always say, 'You did it! That's what matters. And it's good for you.'

Flying has become her passion, just as it is for me. It's what keeps me young and keeps me going. I hope with this book she will inspire other people to find a passion in life that gives them a reason to get out of bed in the morning. It is so important to have a reason to keep going, keep learning and find the joy in life.

If you have picked up this book, I hope you enjoy it, and you too find what gives you the wings that flying has given me and Nushin.

October 2019

Introduction

My life ahead was looking dull and monotone when I discovered the joys of flying. A lifetime of colour and variety in a career in art and theatre had come to an abrupt halt as I moved my mother into a care home. The whole fabric of my life was threatening to dissolve. I felt that people looked right through me; that I had no place in the world and I had left it all too late to make my mark. I had nurtured the hopes and dreams of others, but never my own.

This book captures some of the journey that learning to fly opened up for me. It is a personal story – for those who are struggling to find their own voice in the world, who have disconnected from that confidence of youth, and who are lost in a world where they no longer know what their own desires are.

It was a journey that I often found difficult, frustrating and confusing, but once I had embarked on it, I couldn't turn back. There was the thrill of a challenge so far out of my comfort zone that I always had a knot in my stomach, but I also always felt alive. Alive in every pore of my being. I was finding new ways of being, of looking at the world, of relating to things I didn't understand. I could no longer rely on a version of myself that had grown over years. I had to re-invent myself in the moment.

I also noticed how many other women were locked into grey lives themselves, and that the lessons I was learning in the cockpit were those we all needed in life. This was the journey that led me to become a women's coach, helping others find their own wings and a passion that helped them embark on a new chapter in life's adventure.

This book came from a desire to show others that there is another future out there, if you show up with an open mind and a willingness to take an unknown path. So many of the men I railed against initially became mentors, even friends, along the way, encouraging me to persist. It's not a story of great triumph and enormous wealth, just one of personal satisfaction. Covid and the global pandemic nearly put paid to the whole project, which languished over lockdowns, but it has changed, as I have, over the past six years since I first went up in the air. Nothing, though, changes the profound awe I feel at being blessed with this view of angels every time I fly.

The chapters in the book are based on the syllabus of training for a National Private Pilot's Licence for Microlights. Just as I wasn't your typical pilot student, my training never followed the regular path, it was never a straightforward trajectory. I will never be a natural pilot. However often I am told that I fly well, I need to dig deep within myself to reach those new horizons. But I am proud that I stepped up to an opportunity life offered me and embraced it.

I wish I could tell you it becomes easy, but that wouldn't be true. Yes, it gets easier, but for me, it's always a challenge. A richly rewarding challenge. I invite you, though, to think about what there is in your life that could bring you the joy and satisfaction that this has brought me.

I hope you enjoy reading about how I found my wings to fly.

Nushin Elahi

London, August 2022

1

Pre-flight

Drop a pin – where are you now?

'We're looking for an orange windsock. It's after the church, and if we get to the village of Welton we've gone too far,' said James, as we drove down the winding road that didn't really have room for two cars to pass. Past a tight hedge, with a horse paddock on the left, I suddenly saw it. A windsock fluttering behind a hedge of thorns. The gate was open and the gravel road beyond looked like any farm track. There was a sign: 'Hare coursers will be prosecuted.' What did that mean? I wondered.

I wasn't to know that this was a road I would travel for some years to come, both literally and figuratively. I would be up and down this track, early mornings and after dark, at speed and crawling along, in high spirits and in great trepidation, with music blaring to psyche me up to what lay ahead, and with a knot in my stomach.

That windsock marked a turning point for me – a before and after. Until we turned in at that gate, flying meant nothing to me.

At this point, we weren't there for me at all. My husband James had built, or rather rebuilt, a single-seater plane. It was waiting for someone to test-fly it, and he needed some help. 'Call me if ever you need,' said one of the few people who had known what a Sluka was. We were here to see if he could take it up for its first flight.

The gravel road seemed interminable. A small sign pointed to the left as the road forked, 'Airfield'. The fields looked empty, and we could see a copse of trees in the distance as we crawled along between two fields and then snaked back on ourselves. 'I do hope we don't have to come this way again,' I thought, as the car shuddered in and out of ditches and puddles. I was wishing I had never suggested it at all. Past open fields, village gardens backing onto a stretch of track, a set of barns and what looked like a quarry, it went on forever.

Suddenly, we saw the airfield ahead of us, a few green hangars, another windsock and a small clubhouse propped up on stilts. We climbed the metal stairs, knocked, and opened the door gingerly, not knowing what we would find on the other side. Around a table sat three older men, looking at a stout balding man at a whiteboard. We had obviously interrupted a lecture. They stopped short as we poked our heads in. 'I'm looking for Tom Cartwright,' said James hesitantly. The lecturer pulled himself up to his full height. 'How can I help you?' he asked.

Looking at him then, I could not possibly have guessed that this man would have the power to spark within me a love of flying. There was nothing particularly remarkable about him. And yet, perhaps there was something in how he cocked his head at the mention of flying, in the twinkle in his eyes when he smiled. This man lived his life in a plane, and I didn't know it, but he was about to throw me a lifeline I wasn't yet aware that I needed.

I had come back from a trip, a sort of business trip, to South Africa to a life that was falling apart. I had spent most of my adult life helping my mother with her career as an artist. That involved doing everything that wasn't actually painting the pictures – from sizing, mounting and framing the work, to planning every aspect of an exhibition. It was work I loved. Just like Tom lived for flying, I lived for my mother's art. I was passionate about it. I had written hundreds and hundreds of press releases over decades. I could quote more about her life than she herself could remember. It was my life.

And I had come home to London, after we had packed up her studio, sold what had been our family home and her exhibition space for the past fifty years and settled her into a care home, just like the ones she had always told us she never wanted to end up in. I was bereft. My life, and hers, my career, and hers, were at an end. I wasn't sure how I would fill the void.

It had never been a financially rewarding career. I was always just mother's little helper and, until some of the very last exhibitions, I never really credited what I did as critical to what she did. It took organising a massive retrospective at the city museum and publishing a book about her, for me to realise that without me, none of this would ever have happened. I did it because I felt so passionately about her art, an art that captured the wild side of Africa and brought it into people's living rooms. It opened their eyes to the beauty of nature within their reach, to the fragility of our planet and a world untouched by mankind. I saw through her eyes and helped others do so, too.

On paper, I had been a stay-at-home mum, my career in the arts ensuring that I never hit the high end of salary scales, that I would often do a review for the love of it rather than the pay cheque at the end. My career as a high-flyer had ended as arts editor on a national newspaper when I became pregnant with my beloved daughter Farah. The children were now grown up and largely out of the house. In the intervening years, I had juggled a career around them and a husband who took his work extremely seriously. He was a dutiful provider, but there were many times I would have traded anything for more fun, less duty. Many a weekend away was blighted by a report that needed to be completed before we left, or an email that had to go out while we were away. 'The children won't be little forever,' I kept warning, and now they weren't. The chance to be goofy and kick a ball and hear them giggle had passed, as had so much of our lives.

For someone who never earned much, I had still managed to have all I treasured in life. As a freelance writer, I got to go to theatre shows for the price of a review. I had access to all the art in London thanks to volunteering at the British Museum, and many is the new hip band I got to hear at the start of their career while working at Camden's Roundhouse theatre. I was in and out of every museum in London, seeing a bounty of exhibitions, relishing in the curator's talk at the press opening. I was there for the kids when they got back from school (sometimes only just!), and the first time we ever had ready meals was when we finally decided that snow on the inside of our conservatory was perhaps a sign our whole kitchen needed an upgrade.

Before we moved to London, I was working four days a week at the South African Broadcasting Corporation on their culture channel. It gave me an insight into the world of broadcasting and television. I knew I could have pushed for more, but this way, I could drop the kids at school and connect with my world of art until the school-bell rang. Now that the children were exploring their own career choices, I was feeling slight panic, wondering if this light touch had been a tad too light, if I should perhaps have leaned into my career more actively. At this late stage, my CV would have struggled to fit into any HR department's idea of a dream candidate. I figured I would have to create my own employment, rather than slot into a company. Not being a born entrepreneur, I wasn't sure how to do so.

The financial pressure of two children at university and two mothers in care homes had sent James into overdrive and, with retirement looming, he was working just as hard as he could. I reported on a world of the arts, something that was on a distant horizon to him. He was tense and snappy, feeling the burden of providing weigh heavy on his shoulders. The next chapter in our lives filled me with misgivings. Did I really want to grow old with him? How can you be so lonely next to another person, I wondered? As I contemplated the grim reality of what life without him might look like, the constantly nagging thought was, 'How could I earn enough to keep myself?' Almost everyone I knew in the arts, even those with good careers, was hardly comfortable, and I wasn't likely to achieve any financial stability on my own. I had the material comfort I desired, always having lived on the frugal side of plenty, and the freedom to come and go as I wished. Why did this aching chasm between us leave me feeling so unfulfilled? The children were no longer the glue to bind us, and I wanted to feel I had lived life to the full, not simply gone through the motions and done the right thing.

My mother had lived by her passion for her art. She inspired so many people with her zest for living and the dedication she had to sharing the wonders of nature with her audience. She saw her artistic endeavours as a divine gift, a blessing to share. Once, I was talking to her about the fact that I had chosen this path instead of something more financially profitable, and my mother looked at me and said, 'Oh, but we had fun, didn't we?' What better thing can you say about your life, than you had fun living it? We are given lives to live them joyously, to the best of our ability, not to be ground down by obligation and duty. How could I do that in my own life? I couldn't see the path ahead, yet.

I had a storage container full of paintings of Africa, a house full of books I hadn't ever read, and far too much baggage, emotional and otherwise. Could I step back into a life I could call fulfilling, or was I simply destined to be crushed by boredom and obligation?

2

First Steps – Aircraft Familiarisation

Curiosity and confusion – say yes to life

First flight

'I think you may like to come to Welton with me and see where your dad has moved in,' I joked with the kids one summer afternoon. 'He's never at home now. When he isn't working, he's at the airfield, trying to crack his licence, or make use of the summer weather.'

I had encouraged James to take up flying, I knew. After all, what was he going to do once he retired? Right now, though, it felt as if it had taken over his life. He was working frantically for those dreaded end-of-year tax returns and trying to hand over to his less-experienced successor. Every other spare minute he was up at the airfield, where the Chief Flying Instructor (CFI) was pushing him to get in the air. 'Why don't you all come up and see what it's like?' he had suggested. 'I am sure the CFI will take you all flying if you like.'

We were clustered around one of the outdoor wooden tables, basking in the sunshine. I had met Tom before when he flew James's plane over to Welton Airfield, and Kian had seen him, too, that day. Tom was a brilliant pilot with phenomenal experience – many thousands of hours on every type and in all weather conditions. His enthusiasm for flying, and his can-do attitude were what finally helped James get his little Sluka into the air, and now that same determination was pushing him to finish off his licence. James was delighted with our interest. He proudly introduced us to the pilots passing by, until Tom sauntered over.

'Kian, would you like to come up in the plane with me?' Ever the gentleman, Kian demurred, 'Thanks very much, but I have flown once before, I think Farah should rather have a go this time.' 'You can all have a go!' Tom said, with a generosity I have come to know. I nervously fussed around the plane as Kian got in, checking whether he'd be warm enough without a jacket. 'He'll be fine,' James assured me. When it came to Farah's turn, I took photos and sent them off to her boyfriend. In the air for the first time, it was quite an achievement! My stomach was in a knot, though. My turn was coming. Everything in me wanted to say no. This wasn't my idea of fun at all. I watched the plane twist and turn with Kian inside, and the knot got worse. Farah's flight seemed more sedate, but I could hardly concentrate.

Quarter of a century earlier, long before James and I were even married, James had asked his mate Brian to take me up in his small plane. I knew James loved flying and had once had a pilot's licence, but it wasn't on my bucket list at all. At the end of that day, flying was allocated to the

Never Again pile instead. At Grand Central airfield James was a proud boyfriend showing off his amazing hobby. Any excitement I may have felt was obliterated by the ordeal that followed. I now know that I am incredibly sensitive to pulling G-forces and I feel dizzy very easily. No pilot should have done a barrel roll with someone like me, without giving them a full briefing and checking if they would cope. I didn't. All I recall is the dry dusty Johannesburg heat, and the spinning head that lasted long enough to ensure I knew emphatically that I never ever wanted to fly again.

Now I had to choose. Step into the unknown. Take a chance and find out where it would take me. Just experience what it was like in the air again. Say 'Yes' to a different experience. Or say 'No' and stay in my safe cocoon. My heart was pounding, and my palms were sweaty. My breath was getting shorter and shorter as I faced the inevitable choice.

'Go on!', James and Kian were prompting, as I hovered around Farah, who had just landed and was beaming with delight. 'Hop in!' said Tom. I did. Perhaps I could crush the fear that had lurked in the back of my mind since that barrel roll so long ago. James helped buckle me in and placed the headset on my head. I tried to explain to Tom about my past experience, but he brushed that all aside. 'Oh, stop wittering woman,' he said. 'Just get on with it. By this stage your daughter had it pat. She's a natural,' as I struggled to figure out how one steered a plane with your feet. 'Let's go, shall we? You good? Hold that stick between your legs and push it forward,' as he followed through.

Every first time is different, and Tom is a master at giving every passenger a memorable experience. Too much concern for my sensitivities would have meant we would still be sitting on that runway. There was something in the combination of total command of the situation and delight in his craft that brushed all resistance aside. 'Ready?' was the last thing I heard, nodding dumbly, wishing I hadn't been so foolhardy as to sign up for this. Then the roar of full throttle on the engine took over. My heart was in my mouth as we hurtled down the runway. I am not sure when we parted from the earth below, but suddenly we were aloft, and the ground was sinking away rapidly. We were airborne.

I could see the patterns of the fields unfolding below us. This was the England of storybooks. It was beautiful. 'Want to have a go?' Tom asked in a cheery voice. I took the stick and felt the aircraft lurch and dip dangerously. 'Relax!' he laughed, helping me straighten it out. I only knew he was talking to me because I could see his lips moving and his expressive face. I couldn't hear a single word he was saying. It was like watching a goldfish blowing bubbles.

I had been in big aircraft before. Trundling between London and South Africa, an overnight in the air was nothing new to me. This was different, though. This was what I had promised myself for 25 years that I would never do again. The pilot and I were in a ridiculously tiny tub, piercing through the air.

James had said Tom would take us flying, but I hadn't thought that would mean I had to do anything more than sit and be a passenger. Now I was holding the throttle that was somehow responsible for the speed at which we were travelling. I couldn't figure how it all fitted together. My mind was abuzz with questions, none of which I quite knew how to formulate.

'How are you doing?' Tom asked with a gleam in his eye. My mouth dry, I swallowed, then nodded. The plane turned to the right. We stayed level but changed heading. How did that work? What had he done? He was talking to me, all the time. Cheerful, chatty stuff, about Farah and how well she did, and I must be proud of having such lovely kids. James was doing well and enjoying his flying, wasn't he? I couldn't take any of it in. My mind was in total overload. I couldn't figure what he was using to work out where we were going. And what it was that determined how high we were, or how fast we were heading.

'The aircraft is very stable,' he said, looking at my face of terror. 'It's quite safe. You see, even if I take my hands off the controls, it will just carry on flying on the same path.' He did exactly that. I yelped, 'No, don't!', but only a croak came out. Tom leaned over and pushed the mike closer to my mouth. I was confused. I didn't understand this third dimension. I knew nothing about flying or the physics of what made an aircraft move through the air. I am sure Tom told me a lot about it, but I didn't take in a word. I was in a state of shock, all my senses on high alert.

'We're heading back now, and I think you should do the landing. Both your children did. It will give you something to talk about at the dinner table.' 'Don't be ridiculous!' I felt like yelling, but instead, I managed an emphatic shake of the head. I could see the airfield ahead of us, way below. 'No,' I croaked, then cleared my throat. 'No thanks,' I said more forcefully, 'you can just land the plane. I've had enough. I don't want to do that.' 'Well then, in that case,' he said, turning straight onto Runway Zero Three as he brought us down and taxied back to the clubhouse where my family stood waiting.

The plane came to a halt and the propeller stopped its whirring. I sat trying to take it all in. Those ten minutes would alter the course of my life. As I sat there in the old club training plane, I don't think I realised that I had just taken the first step on a journey that would change my future. That was yet to come.

Second time around

Through all the confusion and fear, something about the visual beauty of that first flight meant I wanted more. It was a third dimension, which opened a whole new world to me, and I was determined to understand it.

'Your daughter is a natural,' Tom had said. 'She really should learn to fly.' Farah was adamant, 'No!' I had to persuade her to share lessons with me. 'Your dad is offering to pay, he has the airfield and the instructor, why not give it a try?' It seemed like a safe enough way for me to take a peek into this strange environment, without too much of a commitment.

We had arrived at the airfield with a cake to celebrate James getting his licence. Huw, a craggy-faced ex-banker with a thick Welsh accent who was friendly and always smiling, was sitting at the table planning his flight for the day. 'One day I want to fly with you,' I heard myself say.

James looked shocked. Where on earth did that come from, even I wondered, but by now I knew fun when I saw it. Huw quickly countered that he only flew with other pilots, a position I now fully understand. Why shouldn't someone earn their keep, listening on the radio, looking for other aircraft, sharing the whole experience? I didn't know that then.

Flying in Huw's flexwing was an almost religious experience. I felt a sense of me, and God's creation laid down in front of me, fields rolling away in every direction, and I was up there alone in it. I could have been an eagle in a clear blue sky. Huw was right in front of me of course, but his headsets didn't really work, and I couldn't quite hear what he was saying, so it felt as if I was alone in this vastness. A flexwing is really a basket attached to an engine and a wing. The bolt that holds it all together is called a Jesus bolt, because, of course, if it comes off, that's who you'll be seeing next! It also involves a lot of kit – putting on a flying suit, which you need to wear about 363 days of the year, most of which are too turbulent to fly in a flex anyway. I speak as a fixed-wing pilot, however, used to sitting in a plane with a heater you can (sort of) control. Those that love flex abhor the confines of a cockpit.

Flying with Tom in the enclosed, fixed-wing aeroplane, I saw the English countryside with its rolling hills, fields with tractors, a little church spire poking up from a cluster of houses, a mansion with manicured gardens, horses in the fields and unused tennis courts. In the flexwing, the cold air was trapped against my skin and the world was laid out around me. Humankind seemed utterly insignificant, it was just nature, and up there I felt part of it. Such a sense of intense wonder, being alone with nothing else around you and feeling quite safe and secure in this tiny basket, was amazing. Seeing the world stretch out forever, suspended in space, was a moment of calm and tranquillity I can recapture forever. It was true meditation.

My mother had felt this, too, in the Namib desert – she saw nature laid out in all its pristine glory. This was not her desert, but I was open and exposed to that endless space, with no sense of the city and its masses of people. I remembered a painting trip I had accompanied her on to the Namib. We were at Kwessiegat, near the Sesriem canyon. The chance of a balloon ride came up, but I let it slip away. What a fool I had been not to have pushed very hard for that experience, I mused now. How could I have let fear stop me from being able to enjoy that floating sensation at dawn in a majestic unspoilt place?

My grieving heart took these gifts of magical beauty as solace and recompense for what I had lost. So much had been taken from me, but I had received these jewels in return.

Lost earring

Why had I said yes, when Tom came over to invite me to take what would be the first step in one of the hardest journeys of my life? When you have an idea of where your life is going, it's easy to take the routes you think will get you there. But I was lost in a maze of dead ends, and felt I had been going in circles far too long. I was stuck. Lost. I couldn't see my way out of the maze and the future I caught glimpses of wasn't bright at all. No, it was dreary and desolate.

Sometimes life offers you a different path, but you won't find it if you don't say yes. 'Yes!' to all the things you wouldn't normally do and try. You are not the same person you were this time last week, last month, a year ago. Why then would you tie yourself down to decisions and patterns you set up decades ago? You may not like what you are being told, but if you listen, and look, you will see that you haven't been abandoned to the scrap heap. You just aren't on the track you thought you should or could be.

We live in a world of exciting options, but we filter out much of what is on offer. I had sat in lecture halls in London, listening to motivational speakers say, 'Judge less, observe more,' as I tried to find a way through my sense of despair at what the future held. At the airfield, I now realised, I was starting to tune into a world of new opportunities.

It was the first time I had arranged a lesson with Tom myself, and I felt annoyed he was fully booked until Tuesday. Still, when James offered to pick me up at the tube station on Friday after my volunteering at the British Museum and let me come up to the airfield with him, I was delighted. I was dressed for going into the city, which for me meant make-up, jewellery, and a pretty summer dress. Wearing pearls and a matching necklace, I looked better than I ever had at Welton. I know, because Ally stopped and commented, 'You look nice!' with surprise, as I arrived. She had only ever seen me in old sloppy jeans and a big fleece, because that's what one wore at the equivalent of a farm, wasn't it?

Ally was a leggy brunette who looked stunning in old jeans herself, or more likely in hot pants, and as a woman coming up for fifty, made all the men's heads turn when she was around. No wonder, she was quite a looker. And she could fly. But only with Tom next to her, or whatever instructor she was friendly with at the time. She rarely came to the airfield now, but when she did, everything stopped for her.

I knew I wouldn't be flying, so I hadn't worried about wearing sensible trousers. Suddenly Tom bounded up. 'I have fifteen minutes if you want a quick flight now,' he offered, 'before my next student arrives.' I was a bit flustered. Bare summer legs and all that. 'Go on, just go, you will be fine,' encouraged James. So, I did, tugging at my dress to make sure I didn't show too much leg as I got in. It doesn't matter what the PC brigade say, there is something satisfying about knowing that every male is eyeing you with approval. Even if you don't really want their attention, it does your ego the world of good, especially when you feel as if your husband looks right through you most of the time. My bright red lipstick couldn't help breaking into a smile.

We set off, for what I now know as a quick hop to the motorway and back, often through some of the most turbulent areas on any flight. It was late afternoon, and the air had smoothed out, as it usually does at that time of day. This was flight number four, so it was all still sparkly and new. I was feeling the cat's whiskers, thanks no doubt to a bit of male attention, including an admiring comment about my looks from the instructor and a bit of banter about taking the controls in a dress. The flight was of little importance but feeling a million dollars made a massive difference to my confidence. Looking good, feeling good, I knew I could do this, and I did. I had dressed for a me that was confident and in her element in the city museum, and that same confidence now translated into this alien environment. I landed the plane back at the airfield – no doubt with a good deal of help – with ease. I had nailed this!

I got out smiling ear to ear, which is probably why James registered that I now only had one pearl drop earring on. I turned and rushed back to the plane where Tom was filling in his logs, hoping I would find the long shepherd's crook nestled somewhere in the fold of the seat, but no amount of scratching made it appear. I wanted to kick myself for wearing something special in the air, but then I thought about the buzz I had from looking great.

It's how you show up, isn't it? I have never been a believer in the 'Fake it till you Make it' adage, certainly not where flying is concerned. If you can't do it, best not to take off at all, I always think. It may have cost me a beautiful pearl, but in exchange I got a pearl of wisdom. Dress for success. I looked good, I felt good, and I knew I could do anything I wanted. Nowadays, when I am debating what to wear, my daughter will say to me, 'Just dress as if you are going to the airfield mum, and you will look fine.' I don't have anything that is too good to wear when I need a confidence boost. And I never went to the airfield without my red lipstick again!

3

The Effects of Controls

Weight, lift, drag and thrust – who's in your life?

The waiting room

I should have known. I used to try calling James a respectable ten minutes after his flying lesson should have finished, only to be told they were still drinking tea and hadn't even got the plane out yet. Later, I'd hear Tom say, 'If you have time to spare, go by air.' It's all true. There's a glacial speed with which things happen at an airfield. There is tea to be drunk – many, many cups – notes to be compared and matters to be discussed. You can't rush these things, as I have found to my cost. Time, it all takes time.

So how did I end up kicking my heels in Tom's waiting room, seething with frustration, I often wondered. I had had a few lessons by now and I knew I wanted to continue with the flying. I had no idea what I was going to do with it but, for the first time in ages, I was having fun – too much fun to let it all go. It came at a cost, financial and personal. I watched the hours – and pounds – clock up with rising panic. It didn't feel as if I was making progress.

Let no one tell you it is cheap to learn to fly. Rather, remember the adage that it takes as many hours as you are old, which would put me into the OAP category! But, as James was happy to remind me, I had started well behind the starting line. 'You took over twenty hours to actually decide you wanted to learn to fly,' he'd remind me when I panicked about how long it was all taking. 'Besides, once you have your licence, it all counts towards reducing the insurance premium.' Ever the finance man!

The clubhouse was a cabin on the edge of the woods. It had seen better days. Grouped around a table were bucket chairs in a variety of colours and states of disrepair. The walls were peeling to reveal the insulation, and if one tried to clean behind the chairs, one found a trail of rat droppings, despite the traps. There was a basic kitchen area, for all those interminable cups of tea. If I had charged 50p for every time I made a cuppa, I would have been able to pay for most of my tuition. At least it was something to do. Besides, I didn't trust anyone else's sense of cleanliness there. Cups generally only got a cursory rinse in a basin of brown water.

Down the corridor, lined with dozens of flying suits of seemingly similar ages to the pilots themselves, was an office and an examination room. The Henry Hoover and I became great friends initially, as I tried to put some order into that back room, even sticking up a rather ironic wrapping paper of a book-lined case to cover an ugly drip in the glue on the wall. I spent many good days trying to clean and tidy, cursing myself for not tackling my own now neglected home with the same vigour.

Sitting around in the room with me, whiling away the hours, was a motley bunch of characters – most of them delightful in their own way once you got to know them. My favourite was Ted, who at 95 then, was everything I thought my mother would be as she grew older. His passion for flying was equalled only by Tom's, and he would come over daily hoping for a few minutes with Tom where he could fly the plane himself. Over the years, Ted has enthusiastically encouraged me when I was ready to give up. He is more stooped now, but his eyes still sparkle, and he almost never turns down the offer of a flight with someone, especially if he is handed control of the aircraft. We have spent many hours talking, not just about flying. I feel I have got to know him as a person too. He inspires everyone who meets him with his sheer dedication to flying. 'It's what keeps me alive,' he always says.

Among the other flotsam and jetsam that sat around hoping for attention from Tom was Nick. Nick was a giant of a man; someone you took up in a plane when you wanted real ballast. He was well into his seventies, and a gentle soul. He loved talking on the radio and liked nothing better than giving you a radio check, or telling you there was no one else in the circuit, the sort of chat that isn't really allowed. He lived with his ailing mum and had to leave promptly in the afternoon, so the carer could leave in time, but he had nothing else in his life. He talked big about planes, ones he'd owned and ones he'd flown, especially acrobatic ones, and I never quite figured out why his licence wasn't current.

Then there was Cicely. Yes, you read that right. As the only women around on a regular basis, she and I should have been buddies, but, when you have been queen bee as long as she had and feel you are being displaced, there is little love lost. Cicely was quite a schoolmarm who managed to reduce me to tears on more than one occasion with her strident tones. Like Nick, she was also in her early seventies, and loudly disapproved of my dress code for the airfield, preferring sensible shoes and big fleece jackets herself. She adored flying with Tom and would come back positively glowing, especially if the weather was very rough. Until I set my sights on getting my licence, she had had no competition and was happy to keep spending the modest settlement from her divorce on her regular slot flying with Tom. No progress report was needed, although she often told us she'd been waiting six months to go solo again since the summer, but a mythical ten knots' wind had been elusive for all that time.

Jack was a soft-spoken, bumbling man, whose other passion was retired greyhounds. He always seemed nervous, rubbing his hands and walking with slightly stooped shoulders. He spoke under his breath in short, staccato sentences. It took me a long time to realise he was simply withdrawn and shy. In fact, it was only when he started liking my photos on Facebook that I knew he had registered my existence at all. He had been working in the aviation industry.

John, a former engineer like James, told us early on that he never socialised with the club members. 'I just come here to fly,' he said. He was a flexwing pilot, and I thought we got along well, but eventually I had to accept he had no desire to socialise with us either. He was calm and precise, able to demystify things for me, but his cool distance eventually translated into detachment.

There were at least five other Johns at the airfield, distinguished by a variety of nicknames. There was Scottish John, Jaguar John because he'd once worked there, Johnny J, Euro John because he flew a Eurostar and Little John, who made up in the speed of his conversation anything he lacked in stature. There was also a Skinny Mike, a portly gent who heaved himself into the confines of any plane; Anxious Andy, often fretting, like myself, about the weather; and the dour-faced Undertaker. I am not sure he ever heard his own nickname, but it was very apt. No surprise that I had a few nicknames myself. I was called Dorothy when I wore brightly coloured pumps, Goldilocks when my hair looked big and curly and Mary Poppins when carrying bags of stuff – headsets, lunch, manuals.

Bert was a strange character. 'Old people and children like me,' he plaintively told someone, 'No-one in between.' A sad summary of a life, but no surprises there. It took me a while to understand why he had never had a partner. He was not unattractive, and it wasn't because of the gammy hip that meant he was officially disabled. But Bert would come out with such obnoxious comments you had to blink hard to make sure you hadn't imagined them. His nasty barbs about other people's landings and contemptuous remarks when others messed up were a facade to cover his own inadequacies. The only flying he did for years was driving the club plane around on the apron.

'If you show your tits to Bert, I am sure he will help you clear the barn,' Tom once helpfully suggested. I was happy instead to pay the young gardener I had brought from home.

Dan started flying shortly after me. Initially, it wasn't obvious that he would become my favourite flying buddy, although his skill as a pilot was apparent early on. He worked for a telephone company and skilfully managed to fit in his work around a busy flying schedule. He was mortified when I took him to task one day for stoking the atmosphere with Tom, when I was finding the constant barrage of innuendos I was subjected to unbearable. It wasn't an ideal start to a friendship, but since then, he has encouraged my flying and given me new perspectives on what a dedicated pilot can achieve.

Then there was the duo who ostensibly ran the club, Alan and Steve. Alan was a cheery man, friendly and caring. He was always happy to engage, and his personal mug said it all: he was there for the flying. His wife never visited the airfield; I think in all the years I have met her once. He had a strange alliance with Bert I could never fathom. They laughed and joked together like schoolkids. I couldn't decide whether it was a plus for Bert or a minus for Alan. Both Alan and Steve worked tirelessly on the upkeep of the club and all that entailed. Steve, although vice-chair, was the real power behind the throne, and regularly clashed with Tom if he didn't agree with how things were running. Incessantly smoking, he had a deep gravelly voice. Tall and thin, he and his batman Micky would pitch up in their van and they'd tackle anything, from the plumbing that was their day job, to building a whole new annex to the club.

Fishy Fred – his nickname acquired from years of working in a fish factory – looked much older than he was, perhaps because his front teeth were missing. He wore sloppy old T-shirts and shorts while his blackened fingernails revealed his status as a mechanic. He had a heart of gold, always gentle and concerned for Ted, taking him flying and helping him figure out the intricacies of technology. It took me a long time to see that heart, though, because what you initially saw was his funny-not-funny opening gambit, 'You getting any? Been under the quilt then?' and a string of puerile jokes about women and sex, the half of which I didn't understand, even if I got the gist of the content. When there were visitors at the club, I sometimes winced at the locker-room banter, and just wished Fred would talk planes instead. When he wasn't around, and Tom forgot to goad me, I eventually realised that most of the club members didn't ever move beyond the topic of flying aeroplanes.

Those were the regulars around the clubhouse table, sometimes popping in for a cuppa and looksee at the windsock, willing to be bullied into the air by their exuberant CFI. There were other fully fledged pilots who would regularly arrive for a flight with Tom. I remember meeting one of them and politely asking where he was in his flying journey, when Tom bounded in and sharply told me that Howard was in fact a licensed pilot. He still only flew with Tom and had done so for the past decade. It was my first inkling of how many pilots needed Tom by their side to enable their flying, just like Ally. I knew I didn't want to join their ranks, becoming dependant on his goodwill for the thrill of being in the air. Every woman he had taught seemed to falter without him in the seat beside her. It was to be a battle theme in our friendship over the years.

In the same way, this was a men's club. The first time James had asked about a family membership, Ben, the flying instructor, asked with his typical cynicism, 'Why would you want that? Most men come here to get away from their families.' 'He's right, they are just a bunch of misogynists,' I snarled at James on the way home, 'they don't want me there.' I had stepped into an alien world. Initially I was quite daunted by a room full of older men with whom I had nothing in common. They would talk about different planes and share their exploits. Even Cicely had many tales of flying with her ex, but woe betide you if you pressed her for any information, as I, with my journalistic nature, was wont to do.

'Suck it and see!' Tom would say when I asked if he had time on a certain day. 'I am sure I will be able to fit you in somewhere, I just don't know when.' I came to hate that phrase. To me, it meant, give up on everything else in your life, come and hang around here talking nonsense with people you don't care about and, if you are lucky, you will go home having done some flying. It also took me ages to figure why he liked having this room full of people who were all waiting to fly. Rather in the way a restaurant only keeps a certain number of places available so there is always a queue outside, it gave an atmosphere of eager expectation in the room. It meant the clubhouse was never empty, like so many others were, but had a bit of a buzz.

I looked with envy at a friendly chap who had been dubbed Forest Gump on day one. He had a slot on a Wednesday morning at 10am and, regular as clockwork, he'd arrive, get his lesson and go. He took a year longer than me to get his licence, but at least he didn't give up on life in the meantime.

Together with the regular pilots who had planes hangared at the airfield, they formed a cast of characters and intrigue that I spent many hours wondering if I could weave into a soap opera for the telly. They were a million miles removed from the traditional view of flying being for the rich elite, bankers and stockbrokers. In fact, I think there was only one former banker amongst them. For the rest, they were kitchen fitters, gas engineers, gardeners, car salesmen, truckers, car mechanics and a hospital porter.

I had never found my own niche in our London life, finding the British reserve almost impossible to penetrate. The flying was giving me a new lift and putting a spring in my step. While I was hugely frustrated at my slow progress and all the hours it took, I was also delighted to find another side to English life. These were real people, who didn't hold back their opinions, who understood the importance of hard-earned cash. They seemed more real than the ones I had met in the city at the theatre and the art museums, and I revelled in talking to them and finding out more about them.

I didn't only make tea for them, I baked cakes and brought them in, I scrubbed the counters down and washed the cutlery. I bought new dishcloths and hand towels. I would defrost the freezer and clear out the stuff growing mould in the fridge.

I remember one evening saying to the two club managers that I would be happy to see if I could raise funds to get some other chairs and make the space more pleasant for those of us who were sitting around in it all day long. Alan looked at me pityingly. 'You will just tire yourself out, you know. You aren't the first woman to have tried to tackle this lot. They just don't care. I sometimes wonder what their own homes must look like when I see how they treat the clubhouse, but they wouldn't appreciate anything you do.' I was surprised, and disappointed.

It was a turning point, for both of us. Not long after that conversation, they started a major project of renovation, so I now fly from a swish-looking clubhouse with its own ladies' loo. I also realised I had given myself a Herculean task, and, like Sisyphus, I would get beaten back. It was emotionally draining enough to tackle the flying; I didn't need to turn it into a home from home. Against fierce opposition, I set up some recycling, but nowadays, Henry Hoover and I are estranged. I sit around the clubhouse like every other pilot, but I do drink out of my own National Gallery mug, so I only have my own germs to contend with.

4

Straight and Level Flying

Have a vision to guide you – the view of angels

Sunlight on the water

'What would you like to do in our next lesson?' Tom asked. I had my answer ready. 'We've been north, south and west. I would love to fly east towards the coast. I worked out that in an hour's lesson we could get close enough to see it and be back in time.'

He smiled. 'It's one of my favourite trips, flying up that east coast. But I think we actually need to go to the beach, and for that we need a good day. Let's put something in the diary. I will take you when the sun is shining. That will be fun.'

I was thrilled at the prospect of flying to the beach. It kept me going through what had been a tough time. My son, Kian, was reeling at suddenly having gone from being a sporty lad to recovering from a major health crisis. It was tricky to support this surly young man who needed help and advice on his new university but was frustrated by his reduced independence. There were times I wanted to yell at him for rejecting the assistance he so clearly needed, but then I would bite my tongue, think of flying up the coast and smile.

I had gone along to Holland to settle Kian into his new digs there. The red tape involved in moving to a new country, especially one where you didn't speak the lingo, was massive. He was still weak after an unexpected operation meant he couldn't fly, so he had to accept mum coming along to carry cases and find where to go. Admitting that he needed help was a difficult pill for him to swallow. My suggestions of how to slot into this city were met with a grisly irritation, and the fact that I could understand Dutch made it even more challenging. Finding his room in Utrecht was only the first step, now he needed to get a bike, to register with the city authorities, with a doctor, to book in for the initiation week. The list was endless.

'I'll be fine on my own,' he said when I first offered to accompany him on the train. Medical advice was still not to fly. Eventually I got a grudging, 'Yes, come if you like,' and booked my own ticket. No young man wants to be reminded of his own mortality. Neither of us wanted this reality. He was fighting his own demons and I was so often the one to take the rap. Sharing the tiny bedsit he was renting meant we didn't get a respite from each other. 'I'll leave early Kian, and spend a night in Amsterdam, if I am so much in your way, shall I?' I didn't, but I did treat myself to a full day in Amsterdam's museums before catching my plane home. I had never visited the Rijksmuseum before, and I revelled in the Dutch masters, before indulging in Van Gogh. I felt I had had a bit of me-time when I boarded for London.

Being on a commercial airliner interested me much more now. I used to hate sitting near the wing, where I could see nothing. Now I tried to see the runway signs as we taxied, listened intently to the hum of the engines as the captain applied full power, and watched the flaps being retracted as we climbed out. Heading into Luton, I saw below what looked like a runway – a long double line of trees with a circle in the middle, so it couldn't be. As so often before, I vowed to find it on a map; this time, I actually did.

Back at the airfield, it was the first thing I asked about. I was intrigued. 'Come here,' Tom called after a few moments' thought, showing me a map on Google Earth. 'Is this what you mean?' 'Yes!' I laughed, 'that's exactly it! What is it?' It was my first sighting of the carriageway at Wimpole Hall which would become a major landmark for me on northbound flights in time. Within a few months I had it marked on my SatNav as a waypoint.

The promised beach day dawned bright and sunny, but I knew better than to assume that meant a good flying day. I got to the airfield and sat feeling that wonderful warmth of the sun on my skin, with a little backpack of a beach wrap, flip-flops and a packed lunch.

When Tom arrived, there was an interminable cup of tea with Andrew, who seemed never to take a breath in his chatter. Waiting in the plane, feeling the wind shake the airframe, I wondered if I was stupid pushing for this beach day that had become a symbol of this hot summer, in which so much had changed for me. What if it was an awful trip and spoilt everything? 'Shall we go and see what it's like up there?' suggested Tom as he jumped in. 'No, let's just go and if it isn't nice, we can come back.'

Today, all I wanted was to feel the sea and sand under my feet and forget about everything else.

There was no real pretence about me doing the flying. This was one of those jaunts where you can learn as much being a passenger as pilot in command. The radio always means there isn't time for chat. It's tricky getting clearance through the Stansted zone, and I watched as even this accomplished pilot obviously had his hands full talking to air traffic controllers. He was talking, writing down numbers, punching others into the radio and still flying the plane. I understood better why all of that made James rather tense.

The countryside below was laid out in its late summer finery, fields newly harvested. I recognised the route, with the boats in the marina, but when Tom pointed out North Weald with its large runway ahead, I could hardly pick it out in the distance. I was frustrated that I still had no idea how he tracked his route and seemed to navigate with such consummate ease; but then, he'd been doing it for a long time. Eventually we neared the coast and the mud flats and salt banks unfolded below. The sun turned the sea into a flat silver shimmer, and I snapped photos madly.

'Get down! Land, dammit!' he muttered as we turned onto final approach over the tiny grass airstrip. 'You see, it's so windy, the plane doesn't want to land.' The beach was only five minutes' walk away, so we strolled over to find a rather typical English beach, with a pier in the distance and a long promenade of eating places. There were steps leading down to a gloriously warm sea, but little shade. I went to paddle, while Tom sat absorbed on his phone.

Later, ice-creams in hand, we sat and watched the mums with their kids, and the gulls swooping down to grab what food they could.

There is something dismal about an English seaside town at the end of summer – the elderly people, the outsized figures, and the tattooed bodies against the inevitable amusement arcade. Kian's first experience of a British beach had been just that, years ago, when we had just arrived in the UK. In fact, it was the next beach up from where we now were. It had been a school trip in March, pouring with rain, so the kids shivered and huddled in front of the slot machines all day, while I talked to the other mums. It was a memorably awful outing. I was surprised Kian didn't ask if we could go back to South Africa, where beaches had sunshine!

This looked the same but felt quite different. I wasn't anyone's mum, minding whiny brats. I was just me, no history, no expectation, just here for the jolly. I had flown here, for heaven's sake, just for the heck of it. The sun was shining and I felt like I had been let out of my cage. I didn't yet know where that would take me, but I was intrigued to find out. I have since flown in with James and landed there myself, but that was the day that marked a vision of a different world. I look at the photo of me in front of the plane and I can see all the excitement brimming at becoming a different version of myself. I was on Cloud Nine, literally.

Flying into a headwind, our trip home was going to take much longer, said Tom, consulting his 'magic machine', as he called his phone. He pointed out the types of clouds above as we walked back, looking at the wind. I only saw little cherub clouds, but he was seeing a change in the weather.

We flew back over the estuary and now all the brown mud flats had turned into spirals of exquisite wonder. The sun was glinting on them, and the sea had started filling up the hollows, which now shimmered in the afternoon light. It looked like an intricate French lace pattern. The whirls and twists of iridescent blue showed the slow flow of the water rising. Everywhere I looked, I saw this tracery, and kept clicking my camera, trying to capture an image of this magic moment.

Memories of grand châteaux and their finery, of delicate lacy fabrics and lush velvets merged and I was looking at artworks drawn on the earth below. If ever I had wondered why I found this journey into the skies so thrilling, I only need to look at those first images. I now have hundreds of photos from so many airfields that are tucked close to pylons near the water's edge but seeing that tracery along the estuary always makes me catch my breath. Tom smiled indulgently at my pleasure, as we tackled the headwind home. Eventually, my gushing must have tired him, and he said, matter-of-factly, 'It always looks like that, whenever you fly there. It's nothing special.' But to me, it was, and always will be. Like a secret code, those whirls of water remind me of a time of wonder.

Red Letter Day

You know how every fancy card has a piece of paper inside, offering you Red Letter Days? You can drive a supercar, go skydiving, have afternoon tea somewhere posh or pamper yourself at a spa. Kian picked up the insert from my birthday card and said to James, 'How about it, dad? Take mum somewhere special for her birthday?' 'That's what I am planning,' James said, with a determined set to his jaw. 'We have an aeroplane. I will take her flying in it.'

I had been learning to fly for nearly eight months now. Correction, I had first gone up in a plane eight months ago. The idea was to be able to fly with James, but I was in no rush. In fact, the more I got to understand about flying, the less rush there was. I knew James was a super safe and sensible pilot, but I also knew just how much could go wrong. I was no longer able to be one of those passengers who has a blind faith in the ability of their pilot. This didn't bode well as a birthday present, but I simply didn't know how I could get out of it.

Bury Hall Farm is a great big runway, a shortish hop from our airfield, with a pub at the end of the village. We had often heard about it as a destination, but today we were going to find out. It was grey and cloudy, but I knew that was probably the best flying weather I could hope for. I wore my bright, happy scarf from Holland and a cosy pink fleece. Inside, my stomach was in a knot. At the airfield, I got little more than the odd grunt of a 'Happy Birthday', which made me even more keen to get this over with. I pulled the plane out of the hangar with enormous trepidation, patting it on the bonnet, the way my mother used to chivvy up her trusty truck when driving into the desert. At this moment, the desert seemed preferable.

I strapped myself in, trying to force a smile. James could probably feel my nerves, but this time he wasn't going to let that distract him. I silently went through all the checks with him as he got the engine going. He was far too good to let my apprehension throw him. We took off on the closest runway and, as we turned over the manor house, I noticed how stunning it was to see it from the air and not have to worry about height restrictions and speed control at this point. The countryside was looking very green under the thick clouds, and the flying was smooth. I consciously tried to unwind and let the tension go. Soon I was able to smile at James and enjoy the pleasure of being a passenger with him.

We trudged across the fields and down some narrow lanes to find this pub, with low ceilings and photos from its American wartime history lining the walls. No pilot can afford to tempt fate with alcohol, so lunch was a sandwich and a soda, clinking glasses to a new chapter in our flying future.

Heading back, I got directions for a path that would lead us straight to the airfield, although walking down the runway took almost as long as the flight there. The plane was tucked away at the bottom of the slope, with white daisies and yellow buttercups sprinkled on the green grass. 'Are we good to go?' James turned to me as the engine reached temperature. I smiled and nodded. I was. It was the first time we had flown together, but, since then, James has taught me so much about flying; he has patiently sat and let me hone my skills while he probably forced a smile and I battled to find my way in this very strange world. That birthday flight was a Red Letter Day, indeed.

5

Systems Failures

Mitigate the risk, embrace the uncertainty

Banished

I was in Bristol Royal Infirmary, sitting by Kian's bedside, a barrage of thoughts whirling through my mind. 'Will my son be okay? Will I ever fly again? Am I a dreadful mother to worry about such stupid nonsense when my son's life and future hang in the balance? Have I completely lost it in the past few months?'

The break with the airfield happened with terrifying suddenness. One minute, I was simply frustrated with hanging around waiting for my lesson; the next, I felt I had been banished. Instead, I was heading down to Bristol to watch my son battling for his life after a routine procedure had turned into something of a problem recovery. Wondering if Tom would ever take me on as a student again, I felt guilty; then I felt guilty about being a neglectful mother. Flying was something I do have some control over, I told Farah, unlike how things pan out for Kian, and the fear of losing something that was so special to me was probably a stand-in for the unthinkable fear of losing my own son.

I had started to feel at home at the airfield, revelling in talking to all the different men I was meeting. When had that ever happened in my working life? In the arts, you can expect the men are looking at the guy you are with, rather than eyeing you up. Suddenly, I was the belle of the ball. I didn't want to look too closely at who else was at the ball, but I was thrilled with the challenge of connecting with guys with whom I had absolutely nothing in common. After years of feeling I had become invisible, the fact that men were looking at me appreciatively made me feel super special, most of the time.

There were other times when I just couldn't swallow the daily sexist comments. 'Oh, it's only fun and banter; you have to be able to take the jokes.' I laughed and smiled, or carried on making tea and pretended I didn't hear that comment, or looked blank because I simply didn't understand the innuendo but knew there was one by the guffaws. Or occasionally, I asked sharply, 'What was that?' to try and shame them into realising just how unpleasant they were making this.

It was a series of unfortunate events that led to the bust-up. My irritation at sitting around waiting all day for bits of flying time, feeling I should have better things to do with my life, was growing exponentially. I couldn't justify the expense of flying lessons; I didn't know why on earth I was doing this except that it was great fun. Most of all, though, I felt I was wasting oodles of time, quite honestly, on people I didn't really want to spend entire days with. My mixed feelings of elation at how I was progressing with my flying were sharply contrasted with confusion about the point of it all. If I were being honest, the sense that I had all the time in the world to hang around, while other more important customers came and went, played right into my insecurities about never having earned enough. It didn't help that I understood I was lucky to be allowed to have bite-sized chunks of flying time, because that was probably the best way for me to process it. I had such a lot of learning to do that long lessons undoubtedly wouldn't have worked.

On the Monday, I had asked Steve, the vice-chairman, about a Facebook post that kept popping up from Martin, one of the other members, offering paid flights in his plane. At the time, that wasn't allowed. 'What did it have to do with you?' Tom would later ask. Nothing, I had to admit, but in a combination of curiosity and indignation at seeing things done inappropriately, I spoke to Steve to find out why that was allowed. 'Oh, you never know what old Martin will do, his plane isn't even ready to fly half the time,' Steve seemed unconcerned. The next day he told Tom about a busybody asking too many questions. The memory stings, but I can see now how I came across as too keen, too curious and, in all honesty, just too much!

The day at the field had been a chapter of bad timings. I had got frustrated waiting for Tom and gone up with Brian Woods in his flexwing, but it took so long to get airborne that we took off to see Tom's surprised face as he came in to land. I spent that flight itching for it to finish, the bar constantly pushing my head forward at an uncomfortable angle that led to a low-grade headache. I was ready for my prescribed lesson time, but the club plane was by now being used by a recent soloist, a child prodigy, who aced it in the same amount of time I hadn't seemed to get much further. He once came back to land and I readied myself for the lesson, but then he instantly took off again and headed out, leaving me crestfallen. When he finally landed, Tom, presumably to punish my cheek at not waiting patiently for him, chose to take Ted up for a quick flip. I sat in the clubhouse listening to Fred make one of his filthy jokes, about women and orgasms. It's branded on my memory of that night.

At the same time James was texting me to say that he was still waiting for Kian to come up from the recovery ward, which should have happened hours earlier, and there was no heating in the hospital. The patient had been kept warm, but James had sat in the freezing cold all day, and it showed in his snappy remarks. Me fretting about whether I was going to get my lesson didn't go down too well. Unsurprisingly.

When Tom and I finally did take off, I had to admit that I was no longer fit to fly, one of the basic tenets of flying. That set an already irate Tom off. 'I have control,' he barked. Soon we were swooping and swirling in low passes over the clubhouse, and with such G-forces that I was begging him to stop, as the headache turned to nausea. It was only the next day he found out about my conversation with Steve, and in a few terse texts, I was told to go to hell.

I was already packing for Bristol, to go and support James, who was buckling under the strain. I had time on the train to sit and reflect on whether I would regret the turn of events, whether I would be looking for another instructor, and whether I would or could actually learn to fly. Maybe

I had been having just too much fun, doing something for myself only, and this was divine retribution for my selfishness. Someone up there, shaking a stick and saying, 'Get back in the kitchen, woman!'

My mind was playing back and forth over the past few days. Phrases such as Brian's 'I need a crash test dummy to go up in my flexwing', or the back-handed compliment that my cute blue and green pumps reminded Tom of Dorothy's shoes in *The Wizard of Oz*, were all part of the pleasure I was finding in being in a foreign environment. They didn't feel belittling, just good-humoured fun that delighted me and got me in touch with the lighter side of my nature. Life didn't always have to be dark, heavy and serious. When the banter turned a bit coarser, though, and I felt I was the butt of everyone's jokes, or they ramped them up just for my benefit, it didn't make me feel so good. Then I would look back and think this break was almost inevitable.

Being with James in a bad mood was miserable. He was so touchy, so put-upon, with the weight of the world on his shoulders, it didn't take much to spark an argument between us. I struggled to deal with it all. I thought of Tom's carefree sense of fun and his determination to enjoy life and wished James had just a bit more of that. Then I thought of the care and concern with which James looked after me, and felt mean. They became the symbols of different lives – one, dutiful, caring, thoughtful and weighed down by life; the other, selfish, carefree and happy. Of course, I knew I was only judging Tom on what I saw at the airfield, and everyone plays a different role at home when the mask is down.

My mother must have had something similar when she threw off the shackles of domesticity to go into the desert and paint, I thought. She would be gone for at least three weeks at a time, sometimes much more, travelling alone to far-flung places. There she would stay in camps, hosted by young conservation officers, not much older than her children, who would take her with them on their reconnaissance trips into the desert. Back at camp, she was expected to pull her weight with everyone else. She used to come back from these arduous painting trips and muse: 'To them, I was only Alice. They didn't know anything about me or my life, they didn't care who I was when I was at home. For that moment in time, I wasn't anyone's wife or mother, I just related to them as individuals.' They were so completely out of her social sphere, they had absolutely nothing in common, except for this passion for the desert where they connected.

It is to her credit, that many of them, and their wives, would look forward to her next visit, and some remained friends throughout her life. They learnt what sort of subjects she was looking to paint, and the next year, would take her to places where they themselves had seen nature the way she did.

I didn't think I was bringing a bit of arts and culture to Welton, but in a similar way, I was interacting with strangers where there was no point of contact other than a shared passion for flying. None of them knew anything much about me and my background, other than that I 'spoke funny'. I was sometimes mercilessly teased for my South African accent but, however often I felt like crying, I had learnt to shrug my shoulders at it. My mother's painting trips were similarly tough. She would always say, 'I had such fun!' but they were never undiluted pleasure. In fact, the more I thought about it, the more I saw parallels. When it worked, the painting just flowed, but there was so much hard work before that magic moment. It was the same with flying. All the angst, the worry, the planning, the up- and down-drafts. Yet, when it was magic, it was hard to beat.

I knew I could be a good pilot. Tom wouldn't have taken an interest in me otherwise. He would get mad at me when I said, 'I don't know what to do!', or when I didn't believe I had done it myself – 'You did it all, what did I do?' But, whatever he said, I knew enough to know that he had smoothed out the landing or stopped me from ballooning. However much I lacked a certain confidence, I also just knew that I could be good at this. It was only my own insecurities that held me back.

Now I was on early morning shift at the hospital. Kian had asked us to be there before the doctors spoke to him on their rounds because he couldn't recall what they had said afterwards. Over 21 he may have been, but there are times parents come in handy. I long ago realised people don't handle pressure the same, and while I fretted about my future flying, James was a bundle of nerves. The alarm went off early because I needed to get to the hospital in time for the doctors' rounds. Only this was the Sunday the clocks changed, so we could have had an extra hour's sleep. James was livid I had woken him.

The night before we'd been to a fancy restaurant on the harbourside, wandering along watching extravagant Halloween costumes and painted faces parade past us. They spilled out of bars, the noise and frenetic buzz as they all sought out the best of times enhancing our sense of alienation. We were wrapped in a cloud of worry and fear, the exhaustion of how quickly things change and the frightening prospect of the future. Would Kian get better, and when? Our flamboyantly camp waiter wrapped a take-home box for Kian to taste some of the flavours of our meal. We went past his windowless room before going to our hotel, trying to tempt him with distractions.

James's frustration felt overpowering, looking at life from a bleak perspective. He was mad at Kian for having his university mates around to visit before we took him home. His discharge only made James more tense and terse, rather than being relieved that Kian was enjoying this time with friendships. He felt ready to explode, and I tiptoed between the two of them, trying to make the peace. No wonder I longed for a place where I was just me. In their different ways, all the men around me exuded disapproval and made me feel I didn't count for anything – from Tom's 'fuck off!' to James's icy cold censure, and Kian's grumpiness. 'It's not the time to worry about flying now,' said a concerned friend. 'You can sort that out at a later stage. Now is the time to focus on your son and get him better.' Of course, I knew he was right.

'Now, I can't pretend this won't hurt,' the doctor said. 'Hold your mum's hand, you will be okay.' They were doing a procedure to try and kickstart the healing. I was watching Kian's face as it contorted with pain, looking at me with eyes growing wider in horror, trying to breathe. He tapped his throat to indicate he couldn't get oxygen, convulsed in on himself. Who knows what would have happened if a young Yugoslav doctor hadn't come in and talked him through the crisis, distracting him while the morphine kicked in? Or the time when the stitches were coming out and the nurses suddenly realised they needed a doctor to knot the gaping hole. As they dashed out, I sat holding the drain in place, keeping the conversation going so we didn't talk about what was actually happening in the room. When the bearded Spaniard arrived, he did his stitching with aplomb, telling Kian he could be proud of his scars. 'Yes, I'm debating between a shark attack or a lion,' Kian joined in the merriment, while I felt the tears well up inside. Would I ever attain that unbearable lightness of being that was the title of a book a boyfriend once gave me? Did life have to be a drag? Was my glimpse of fun just a flicker that had died?

How to make yourself unpopular – again

It was a miserable January morning when I rocked up at Welton, believing I had been bidden to attend by Tom. A television crew was coming to interview Ted for a test episode on old pilots and Tom wanted the club members around to show their support. 'Where's James?' he barked, when I arrived alone. I should have taken that as a warning, but I didn't. James was summoned and was on his way.

I was in my element, happy to connect with the freelance crew, chatting about the difficulties of working in the UK and wondering if I could do any ongoing work with them. I offered to help with the actual shoot, so, when the room was cleared and everyone trooped out, I stayed put. There were three ladies there – Cicely, Ally and Sarah, Tom's partner – who were dispatched to buy biscuits. I could just imagine how I featured in the conversation in that car. I didn't care. I was sitting opposite Ted, so his replies were more conversational. At one point Tom walked back in, just as I was prompting Ted, reminding him of an incident he'd told me about. Tom hissed at me to let Ted do the talking and stalked back out. What he would have given to throw his weight around and get me out of there, I later realised, but I was far too caught up in the moment to even register. I was delighted at being on known ground for once, cameras rolling, making sure it all went well.

Outside, of course, the temperature was reaching boiling point. Tom was apoplectic, scarcely managing to remain civil to me in front of the visitors, while I prattled on, filling them in on the back-story of flying. The three ladies were incandescent at being relegated to providing refreshments, while I was ensconced inside. Ted quickly realised which way the wind was blowing too and complained to Tom that I had told him to put his cap on when he went outside.

I never saw the final footage, but I would love to watch with the clarity of hindsight. I had been in my own bubble of delight, happy to have been one of the chosen few to be included in the shoot, and blissfully unaware of the hurricane storm I was creating around me. More sensitive to the weather, my long-suffering husband offered to take Ted out for lunch at the local. 'Thanks, I won't go,' said Ted, realising that aligning himself to us would not be a sensible move.

'I don't even think you understand what you do,' said Tom, when I called to apologise later for upsetting anyone. He then proceeded to tell me how every member of the club had complained and disliked me and my actions intensely. If I had thought I was part of the gang, I hadn't read the situation at all well. No surprise then when I got a text saying we'd leave the lessons until I got back from South Africa. Even I could understand that they may not happen after that either. I was bewildered and confused, then enraged, then worried. Tom was still the key to my flying; I needed his enthusiastic support to stay airborne. He gave me the confidence to feel I could do it. Without him, I didn't really believe I was able to fly.

'Let's try some flying in South Africa,' suggested James, always calm and able to see a solution, at least for others. I spent my first night in Cape Town writing a letter of contrition, livid that my newfound pleasure could be taken away from me by some chauvinist. 'Oh, great lord and master of the air, forgive thy handmaid's transgression and restore her to the chamber of thy bounty!' was my infuriated midnight scrawl. The problem was, he probably didn't get irony, and would think I was sorry, when I was simply angry. At him, for being such a controlling dictator, and at myself, for not having the gumption or the confidence to flounce off and find a better solution. I had eaten humble pie after Halloween, now it seemed it was on the menu once again.

6

Climbing and Descending

Focus, meaning, action

Going home

Table Mountain in all her glory. The Mother City, nestled around her folds. The blue sea lapping at her shores. Not a cloud in sight. And here I was, in a small cockpit, eyeballing this iconic view of the country of my birth. I had to pinch myself. This had to be a dream I didn't even dare to imagine come true. This was flying and it was as majestic as the scene in front of me.

I only had seconds to register it. Fortunately, I was brave enough to mutter a 'You have control' to the instructor, whip out my phone and capture an image that I still treasure. I was getting used to incurring the wrath of flying instructors. A few days earlier, I had experienced total banishment from Welton. Now I had another disapproving instructor by my side. And I was paying for the pleasure. I wondered why I did this to myself.

Just when you think you are on top of something, certainly in flying terms, along comes something else that knocks you off your perch. It's the updraft and downdraft phenomenon. You are constantly climbing and descending in the air. The chance to fly in South Africa was just one such for me. I had 25 hours under the belt now, enough to feel like I knew a bit about being a pilot. That's all some of the young university lads have when they take their test, for heaven's sake.

Flying in South Africa

Fanie was a friendly, chatty Afrikaans chap, and we had hit it off on the phone. I love speaking in Afrikaans when I am able. It reminds me of another life, and all the things I handled with ease and confidence. 'Early morning, before the wind gets up,' his wife had suggested. So, we trailed across the peninsula in peak rush-hour traffic to get there. James was wonderful, so supportive, so soothing when I fussed about money, or hassle, or whether I would cope. 'It will do you the world of good, to get another take on flying. See how they do it here. Don't worry about how much it will cost, just enjoy it.'

We had time to take a good look around before Fanie landed. Every type of aircraft there – from GA planes to microlights and gyrocopters. And more women flying than I had ever seen in the UK, I thought as I taxied behind a pretty blonde girl. The plane was different. Everything was different. There was a formality about it that we certainly didn't have at our little farmer's field. All the instructors were in white shirts with epaulettes. This was serious stuff.

Our telephone conversational ease was forgotten. 'All aviation is in English,' Fanie said, as I tried to explain I didn't know the flying terms in Afrikaans. He was nothing if not thorough. We went through all the checks – from filling in a weight and balance form (at least I hadn't been made to get on a scale at Welton!) to collecting the plane's papers ('What if we get stopped by the authorities as we land?') and then walking around the plane to check it. Inside he showed me how the controls worked, telling me about the stall speed on the plane. The throttle was on the left, it had toe brakes and you had to use the rudder. 'Just like the Ikarus,' he said, 'just the same as every plane.' But it wasn't. I was used to flying with the stick, hardly knowing what the rudder did, and this plane – admittedly like most others – was all rudder work, which meant you used your feet all the time. The throttle was also one of those push-pull levers, rather than a long arm I was used to. More than once I was closing it when I should have been pushing it forward for full throttle.

'Where are your safety drills? Pre-, during and post take-off?' Why couldn't I keep the plane at a steady height? There I was, drifting up until we were going to bust the zone. And circuit patterns? Didn't I understand about keeping height and then descending on the base leg? And right rudder? I let the plane pull over until we nearly hit the trees on take-off. 'When there's a problem, you must do something to fix it. You can't just sit there and wait for the instructor to sort it out!'

Fanie went through his checks, none of them the British acronyms, and I asked in a plaintive voice, 'Will you do the take-off? I don't think I can get my head around the controls.' 'That's fine, you just follow me through.' We took off and did a big circuit. I asked about how you come in to land. 'Just like every other airfield in the world, you fly overhead, then descend on the dead side and join the circuit.' Not the farm strip where I have been learning, I thought. This was just an awful waste of time and money. 'At what speed do you take the wheel off the ground?' He went off pop about people who get taught by numbers. 'You have to feel these things, to hear when the revs are right.'

I didn't feel scared, but quite bewildered, and as we flew out of the circuit, he gave me control. It didn't help when I suffered brain freeze about the throttle. 'Aim for that *koppie* and we'll head out to sea. Now you are too far over to the left…' and so it went on. Then I turned and could see the magnificent outline of Table Mountain ahead. Fanie had been totally dismissive when James said, 'She likes to take photos.' 'She must decide if she's flying or going for a jolly.'

Every time I now look at the photo I took on that flight, I am pleased I did that. When will I ever be there again – flying myself towards one of the most iconic images of my country of birth? Fanie gave me no chance to relish the moment. 'Keep behind the breakwater, we don't want to go over the built-up area. No, not too far out, I don't like sharks!' As we got closer to the mountain, he called up Ysterplaats, the military airbase, to get clearance, and was then annoyed when I decided to turn around and go back. The thought of turbulence around the Cape Town harbour area was more than I could cope with. I was also watching the Hobbs meter ticking up and wondering just how long it would take us to get back. James and I had only budgeted for an hour's flying.

Heading back, Fanie suddenly said, 'Well, you are getting the hang of this now, but at base it almost felt like you had never flown before.' There was no stroking of any egos here. I certainly wouldn't have got going with my flying if I had started out like this. This was more like hard work than fun, but I knew it was probably just what I needed at that moment.

Two hours later, I got in the car and could hardly hold back the tears. I had started my lesson cock-a-hoop, cheerful and confident of my abilities in flying. Yes, I had a way to go, but at least I knew enough to know I wanted to learn to fly properly. Now the only thing I knew was that I may have been having fun so far, but I knew nothing – not about flying that is. I sat silent for ages, taking it all in, feeling utterly mentally overloaded. Then I lifted my chin. I hadn't done too badly after all. It was a strange plane, in totally different surroundings and I hadn't flown for a while now. Without James I would have felt like I hadn't achieved anything. I did wonder if I had just wasted all that money, but actually, I decided, it was a good thing. I would be better prepared for the Skyranger with this experience.

Tom had got me in the air with his enthusiasm. Now it was time to get down to the nitty gritty and learn the drill. James was right, a new perspective could only help. I cursed Tom in my head that day and in the following days as we did a few more hours. 'He's stealing your money!' exclaimed Fanie. 'Just helping a little bit here and there so you don't know what you are doing wrong. You don't fly like someone who has over twenty hours – more like five hours. These guys just want to keep their plane rolling, so they help a little, especially with the feet, and you think you can fly, but you can't. Flying is expensive. You must understand what you are doing.' It was a blow to my ego.

Did Fanie love flying? Was it a thing of wonderment to him? I never found out. He wasn't interested in the beauty of it all. He was teaching a skill, not inspiring a passion for the wonder of flight. If this is what I had experienced at the start, I would never have embarked on my journey. I may not have had the finesse or the procedural knowledge of aviation, but without the joy and delight, that vision of angels Tom had shown me, I would never have come back for more. Every time Tom makes me mad, I place that against his transgression. It is a debt of gratitude like someone saving your life.

At night I lay in bed listening to the wind they call the Cape Doctor blowing and wondered if the next day's lesson would happen. When James had asked Fanie what weather apps he used, he got the answer we still quote: 'I look out of the window and see what the weather is doing.' It doesn't really work in the UK though, where the weather changes from one hour to the next.

The next lesson left me frustrated. I spent half of it sitting on the runway unable to control the plane with the rudder pedals and line it up straight for take-off. Eventually Fanie took over, but I figured I could have used his time to better effect if we had been working in the air. The lesson was about circuits and their rules, more than I had ever had at Welton. Soon my head was buzzing. I was ready to quit, but we did another circuit – perfect shapes on my Skydemon, but Fanie wasn't happy with my checks or my use of the pedals.

'Have you ever done a dead stick landing?' he asked. This is what every pilot dreads, when your engine cuts out and it all goes quiet. And it is what you are meant to keep practising, so an engine failure doesn't mean you're a goner. 'Yes, but not with no engine, just the throttle set to idle.' 'That's not a real one,' he said scornfully. 'You need to feel what it is like when the prop isn't turning at all.' He issued instructions on the radio and the circuit was cleared for our descent. Even writing this I can feel my neck hairs rise. What if something goes wrong? Practice forced landings are part of the training syllabus, but deliberately cutting the engine means there is no chance to power up when you have misjudged things. It is an exercise in handling an emergency that can turn into an emergency itself, and more than one pilot has lost his life rehearsing the crisis.

We were both quiet as Fanie brought the plane in to land. The silence was deafening. The concentration intense. His circuit was exact, handling the plane now as a glider, and able to judge accurately just how he could bring it in to land. No chance of 'a trickle more power' to get you over the trees at the edge of the runway. Not something to try if you don't have a good long tarmac runway to practise on.

An hour of ground-school learning afterwards left my head throbbing. And then Fanie did a very clever thing – he made me write my own progress report to give to my instructor. I never did show it to Tom, but it made me assess what I had learnt and what I still needed to learn. We planned another lesson, but the South Easter wind put paid to that. I left South Africa understanding that flying over its often dry and dusty plains was a lot less attractive than the patchwork fields I had become used to in the UK.

A new challenge, another instructor?

Something else was brewing then which took up even more of our time. James had seen a good buy online and set things in motion to get our own aeroplane, the wonders of technology meaning it didn't matter that we were on the other side of the world. It was a sporty Skyranger Swift, with a 100-horsepower engine, faster and nippier than the C42 Ikarus I was currently learning in. Tuition in one's own plane costs half the price of a school plane. Things moved quickly, with Tom back in the UK discussing the delivery with the owner's CFI. Flying is a small world – everyone knows everyone else. It was a bit like, 'my guy will pay, what sort of plane is your guy selling?' By the time we got home two weeks later, our new plane was waiting in our hangar. James's single-seater had been banished to an outside stand.

It was lucky it all happened so fast I didn't really have time to call a halt to it. An aircraft is a rare breed of vehicle that increases in value, so you aren't likely to lose money on it. You are probably going to be able to sell it at pretty much what you paid for it, despite the many hours of fun you have had flying in it. It did change my situation, though. Tom had always promised he would teach me to fly if we got our own plane, but I wasn't sure he still felt that way. Ted and I were back to being the best of mates now, and he assured me Tom didn't harbour grudges, but I got back from South Africa to a very chilly reception.

Would Tom in fact teach me to fly, or should I be looking at alternatives, I worried. 'Stick with him,' said Huw, 'he's the best! All instructors have their issues, but everyone thinks Tom is a god. All the other flying people think he is wonderful.' 'Perhaps, but he just doesn't like me.' 'He can't handle you. It's the South African thing. I've worked with Australians and South Africans. They are different. They come back at you, it's just how they are, and he's not used to that.'

Driving up to the airfield, knowing I wasn't wanted or approved of, I felt horribly flat. I didn't know if I ever wanted to fly, not just today, but ever. 'What if you felt like this when you had adopted a baby, didn't know if you even wanted to be a parent?' I asked James. 'Well, at least with this one we can send it straight back to where it came from,' he laughed. I was ready to cry. Turning off the motorway, I felt a huge wave of relief as we saw the club plane flying out. It was the first time I had been back since the day of the interview. Tom would be out with Cicely for the best part of an hour, which meant I could go in and say hello to everyone and we could meet our new baby, the Skyranger. Known as India Alpha, it was a little beauty.

There were a couple of snide comments from Tom as he came towards us later when James was taking photos of me at the plane, but he did offer to take me up in our new plane. As we were going up, Dan came over, laughing, 'You going flying? Going to take her up and abuse her?' 'Yes!', said Tom, and Dan looked at me, 'I meant the plane.' 'I didn't!' said Tom with feeling. It wasn't the best start to a flight I would happily have passed on entirely. If it hadn't been our plane, and I knew I must give it the best chance, I would have suggested we go home early. Tom was very formal, and abrupt. No chit-chat, no 'how was your holiday?' I said nothing to him either. 'It's going to feel very different,' he said, 'everyone who starts out with a C42 hates the Skyranger at first, then ends up loving it. It's a much better plane, but it does take some getting used to.'

'So, what do you think?' he asked, as I struggled to even get the plane started. 'I agree with what you said,' I replied. I certainly wouldn't have satisfied Fanie, no straight white line for me, but I think all Fanie's carping on about steering the plane and using the rudder, those four lessons that had made me feel so dreadful, bore fruit that day, and meant that Tom was quite gobsmacked at my flying. As I taxied down to the runway, relieved that I had made it off the apron without clipping the wings and wondering if I should slow down with the brakes, I felt I was managing quite well. Still no white line to stick on, but it didn't feel like the first day in Cape Town. I'm certain Tom helped me straighten it on the runway, but I took off effortlessly, just easing the plane into the air, not bringing the nose up too high. 'You did that better than James!' he harrumphed.

Turning away from the airfield, I looked around and couldn't help smiling. 'It's amazing! It's wonderful!' I felt at home, I felt I could do this pilot thing, and I looked at him and laughed. I can't really say he smiled back, but perhaps he softened a bit. I had been worried it would be bumpy up there, because the clouds had built up, but it was quite smooth. Every now and then I'd say, 'Was that you?' when the plane swerved a bit. 'No, it was a bump in the clouds,' he said.

It was beautiful, the sun was streaming down, the fields looked green and lovely, and I really felt I could do it. And so I did! When Tom said, 'Let's turn back here,' I asked, 'Can't I carry on a bit?' Then as we crossed the motorway, he took the plane up higher, and showed me rudder co-ordination, and I played around going to the left and the right. Suddenly I had had my fill. We came back into the circuit, and he was very sharp about stick and rudder. 'You are going to do this better than James if it kills me,' he said angrily, when I couldn't manage to land. On final approach, I fumbled, took my hands off for him to sort it out, and he yelled, 'I didn't say I had control, you'll bloody get this right!' So, we went round again, and again. 'I think I did amazingly!' I crowed when I finally landed, to which he muttered, 'I must agree.'

I didn't say it, but it was all thanks to flying in South Africa, which I had told him about it somewhere near the water tower. 'Oh yes, how did you get on with that?' he had asked. 'It was awful, I hated it.' And so I had, but now I saw the effect. The flying was such fun I thought Tom would surely thaw, simply because if one person in a tiny space is yelping with delight at how wonderful things are up there, it's hard to be in a big sulk. I was so very grateful that I flew well, I wrote to thank Fanie, because it meant that Tom had to take me seriously. I knew that if he didn't believe I was a very good pilot, he wouldn't be prepared to teach me.

Saturday was spent at Old Warden, in the company of the delightful Ted, who took me there on a very roundabout route, was the star of the show and offered us some stale small cakes when I brought out sandwiches at lunch. He told me that Tom had said I was flying well. 'He said that in a crowded fish and chip shop, in front of other people, so he must have meant it. I told him it must be because she has a good instructor.' The wily old Ted is always keen to keep on the right side of Tom!

The next day, I realised that if I had thought things were easing up, I was so very wrong. We went up to the airfield, James hoping to go up in the Sluka, but the winds were too strong. James was outside and busy most of the time, but I was chatting to all the guys inside when Tom and his partner Sarah walked in. Tom had a stonking cold. He barked at me, 'Is James flying today?' 'He was hoping to, but the wind is so strong he decided not to go up.' Soon Tom was having a barney with someone about insurance, then suddenly he turned on me, 'How did you get on at Old Warden yesterday? Ted said the chairs were uncomfortable.'

There was a lot of banter about winds and wimpy pilots between the instructors. Suddenly Tom turned to James, 'Would you like to go up now? We can go and have a bash.' 'No thanks, I think the wind is too strong, I'll pass.' I was at the kitchen sink and came towards them. 'I'm game to fly now,' I said. Tom didn't answer me or look at me at all. There was total silence for a moment, then he said to Ben, 'You want to fly James's new Skyranger, Ben? You can take Nushin up.' Ben didn't react, but I was livid. How dare he! I wasn't going to be passed on from one instructor to another like a piece of smelly fish. James carried on drinking his tea, and I motioned to him, 'I don't want to!' Ben ignored everything. I have since discovered it's the way both instructors handle tricky situations, they ignore them. Nothing more was said, and we left as soon as we could. Sarah still sweetly said, 'You going? Not flying then?' 'No,' I smiled through clenched teeth, as we walked out, waving goodbye to Tom who was by now talking on his phone outside the room.

I looked at him that day and wondered what I ever saw in him. He was so rude, so cantankerous, snapping at Sarah, too, just a thoroughly unpleasant character. What had happened to the person I thought was my friend, who was caring and thoughtful and quite charming, full of enthusiasm and warmth? I wasn't prepared to be humiliated on this scale. It was as if Tom was trying to drive a wedge between me and James, too, by ensuring he stayed ever so pleasant to James, while blanking me. It was way beyond anything I had ever experienced, and I believed it was a determination to crush my will to bend to his. There was no possibility of a meeting of equals. It all had to happen on his terms. I wasn't sure when the one version of Tom left the room, and the other entered, but until now I hadn't understood. This wasn't a man I wanted to have anything more to do with.

My sister said, 'Just ignore it, keep going and act as if nothing has happened, and eventually it will go away.' James told me not to ask Tom for anything, or put him in a position where he could say no. 'Just be polite, and don't try and be his friend. You brought it on yourself by asking to be taken up. Wait to be offered a flight.' 'Perhaps I should see if I could do that for Lent – give up asking for anything,' I muttered under my breath. I was dead keen to learn to fly the plane and get my licence, and at that moment, Tom had us in a bind. We had a plane and no instructor without him.

I had been so happy at the start of the year when I had finally secured a regular slot with Tom. For once, I now didn't need to keep in constant contact and be begging for a lesson. No, now I could just arrive like Forest Gump, at the allotted time, and go flying. Except it never worked out like that. There had been one or two lessons before the television fiasco when Tom blew his top at me, and then on my return from South Africa it just happened that Tom wasn't around those days. 'Nothing to do with you, but I can't make it.' He never offered me another day, rather suggested I go up with Ben, who conveniently had time between jobs and was at the airfield all the time now. I imagined it would be a temporary arrangement. One day James looked at me texting Tom to say I couldn't make that lesson. With all the care and affection of someone seeing a dear one hurt themselves, he said, 'Tom hasn't got you in his diary anymore, my love. He's not planning on flying with you. You needn't bother letting him know. He doesn't care whether you have a slot with Ben or Marco.' I was crestfallen, but I knew he was right.

Tom had got me in the air, but he wasn't going to be the one to help me get my wings. I had to make another plan.

The one that got away

Instructors are like runways. They each have their own quirks, and you won't know just how tricky they are until you land there. Strangely enough, I would never have become a pilot with either of the women instructors I have met. James started learning with Gillian, a highly intelligent woman, who, the first time we met, had made a perfectly simple concept – the difference between measuring height from the airfield or from sea level (between QFE and QNH) – so complex that it instantly fried my brain. It took me ages to figure it out for myself. Nowadays, if I ever meet her, she immediately reduces me to that same level of understanding, despite my hours as a qualified pilot. And the other woman? Well, she was so timid, I would never have trusted she could save me from myself if I did something stupid in the air. That probably explains why all the instructors I know would most likely admit to having egos the size of a house. The students make them feel they're a god, and they forget that that ends when they close the hangar door.

I fell in love with the magic of flying, not the technicalities. That I learnt when I was totally hooked on the thrill of being in the air and realised it was what I needed to be there. The skill came long after experiencing the vision of how flying could transform my life. Yet skill is what most instructors sell. The Fanies of this world will teach you all the safety checks you need, but you need to bring the inspiration yourself.

Marco is the only other instructor I have met that sold passion as part of the package. He had an ease about him, the same enthusiasm for flying Tom had. I liked him immediately. I figured if we fell out, we'd have a good row and move on as friends. He was often at our airfield, despite running a few himself, because he was also an examiner.

He was a great bear of a man with a hug that enveloped you entirely. He was prone to bursting into operatic song in the cockpit. He and Ben were both Tom's protégés, constantly in touch throughout the flying day, but they couldn't have been more different. Marco was warm and open, his Mediterranean background meant that you could just as easily catch him mid-aria as get an overblown bollocking. Secretly, I think the reason was Marco's wild youth, when he took loads of youngsters on those package holidays and had an uproarious time with them. Marco was a great one for throwing parties, and his airfield was the place to go for a loud and boisterous Christmas party, while Welton didn't have any club spirit at all. He was also one of those gentle giants, his own personal vulnerabilities meaning he had great compassion for others when he cared to show it.

I often wonder what sort of pilot I would have been if I had followed my instinct and left Welton and gone up to Marco's at Fiddler's Green. I think I would have been more confident, less insecure in my abilities and it probably would have taken just as long to learn. I was close enough to going solo in the club plane it wouldn't have taken me too long to pass my test and then I could have started to convert onto the Skyranger. Instead, I went from close to going solo, to right back at the starting blocks, rather like a game of Snakes and Ladders. With its powerful engine, our plane was a bit like being close to driving a Morris Minor and then switching to a sportscar.

That was my chosen option – fly up to Marco's place and learn there. James could just get up to speed in flying the new plane, then he could take me up to Fiddler's Green to learn. It was cheaper by half in our own plane, and if I learnt in Marco's C42, not only would we pay more, but I would then have to transition once more to our Skyranger. James flatly refused that option. 'It doesn't make sense,' he insisted. 'I can fly you there, you get your lesson, and I fly us home.' I tried hard to make it work. The only problem was the weather. It never played ball. I made one booking after another, and each time we decided to cancel.

Logistically, I had to accept that the most sensible option would be to accept Tom's suggestion and work with Ben, however cynical and sharp he seemed. My impression of him was of someone who was bored with the tedium of teaching stupid students the same thing over and over. Having now spent many hours in a plane with him, I still don't feel we have ever really bonded, but I do know I learnt an awful lot from him. Right from the start, he said to me, 'You want to get your licence or not?' 'I do,' I replied. 'Then we'll do it as I say.' There was no further discussion. If ever I started to say, 'But Tom told me…,' I would get sharply told, 'I'm not interested in what you and Tom did in 1948, this is what I want you to do now.' This certainly was a new chapter in my flying.

7

Take-off and Landing

Rinse and repeat – clarity through repetition

Three months in the circuit

'For the purposes of this exercise, I am your granny. I don't like to be shaken about, I don't like my fillings rattled or my wig to come off. I don't want to go too fast. Nice and gently now. Let's go!'

We were taxiing down to take off on Runway Two Six when Ben declared his alter ego. I was laughing at him and thinking how good it was to feel happy and relaxed when flying, rather than have Tom's almost tangible dislike of me fill the cabin. To be fair (Tom's favourite phrase), he probably didn't think anything at all, but for me, there was such a vast chasm between his early friendship and his current surliness, that it made me tense and anxious. And that doesn't give you the uplift you need to fly.

Ben stopped me short as I rattled through the safety checks. 'What does that mean? Doesn't help doing something if you don't understand why.' He sounded abrupt and irritated, and I stammered over my answer.

'You're just stirring the pot with the stick. Are those ailerons working? Look left, look right.' I looked at him with surprise, and a new respect. He had always struck me as something of a show-off, who loved to push the boundaries of what a plane could do, yet here he was making sure I got to grips with the details of these safety checks. When I asked if I should use flaps today, he sat blank and stony-faced. Quickly, I corrected myself. No questions here. I was captain of my own plane. 'I'm here to sit and be bored. You're the one flying the plane, not me. I want to do as little as possible. Soon I won't be here, then you must decide for yourself, so do it now.' 'You're just mean, Ben,' I had said in that first lesson, when he wouldn't answer me, but I was used to it now. It didn't make things easy, but it was teaching me to be independent.

For as long as I could remember, I had been terrified about flying without Tom, or with anyone but Tom. It was what always riled me about him, that he had such power over whether or not I flew. If he withdrew his support, I would be left stranded on the ground. And then he did; so comprehensively I had to look elsewhere. But in the process, he had opened up flying for me. Now I had flown with Marco, Pete, Neil, Ben and even Fanie, who had questioned why I seemed so hopeless with the procedural side of flying when I had been doing it for so long. They were all different, and each one gave me a nugget or two that helped me in some way. It was about moving from being a student to being the pilot in command.

'Do you see how much nicer it is when you keep it in that tight little box? You only shook up my wig once,' said Ben, as I came in to land for the third time. 'No more of that epilepsy that I saw on the first day, with all the flapping, and effing and blinding. Just quiet and calm. I want to feel safe. I may be your granny, but I want to go quietly in my bed one day, not on the runway as you jump around and pull the stick backwards and forwards.' He took over from me. 'I have control. Follow through with me.' As we came in to land, he swung the stick back and forth, making me feel quite queasy. 'Am I helping by thrashing the stick around? Is anything easier if I whack it to and fro? Will it help save Johnny and all the little children in the orphanage who may be taken out if you don't land properly? No. Will it help stop the nuclear war that will erupt if you smash into that bunker? No. So just relax and enjoy it. One more and then we'll stop for a cup of tea,' he finished, as he handed control back to me.

Exercise 12 and 13

The circuit. I felt as if I had been locked in the circuit for months now. All Ben and I did were circuits – take-offs and landings. 'That's the stuff that will kill you, so you had better get them right,' encouraged my friend Dan. Perhaps, but wasn't variety the spice of life? Did I have to do that to the exclusion of all else?

'Oh, stop your whinging,' barked Ben. 'Get in the plane and let's go. Have you done your safety checks?'

'It's all pitch and power. Your speed is all over the place. Get the speed right, and the landing will be easy.'

'So, what went wrong there? It was fine until about two feet off the ground, then you just decided you wanted to get the plane on the ground as quickly as possible and you smacked it down. Let's finesse it a bit, shall we? Off you go again.'

And again, and again.

'That was good, now give me three more like that, and we can do something else.'

'I'm going to charge you five pounds every time your speed goes out of that arc. Keep it constant. No, it's way out of control.'

'You can't go bashing about like that. What's the point of climbing up so high, at a million miles an hour, and then you come screeching in, hoping like hell you can get it down on the ground.'

'Now you just dragged me over the hedge. We nearly ended up in the cornfield. I want you a quarter of the way down the runway.'

'What happened there? You panic about some guy on the radio, who isn't even anywhere near us, then you lose focus as we come in, don't want to land on the dogwalker's head, and we run out of runway!'

'Right, I want a nice, controlled, tight box. Remember, when the wind is crashing about like this, you must keep everything under control.'

'Remember, when there is no wind, there is no margin for error. You need to be exact.'

'Relax, take a deep breath. Stay coming down.'

'I'm not going to answer your questions. Soon I won't be here, and then you will have to make decisions on your own.'

'Do what you like. Don't ask me.'

'You're flying really nicely, when you give yourself the chance and stop faffing about.'

One day, I promised myself, when I had the option, I would fly over the pylons and out into what was called the playground. And only do a single landing when I came in. One day. For now, I was locked down here. Gritting teeth was pointless. Instead, I smiled at the prospect of going it alone.

That phase of my learning lasted three months, and a very dull three months it was. I would have done anything to take a break, shake things up a bit. I still believe I would have learnt much quicker if Ben had taken my suggestion, let me fly somewhere else and tried landing there. There are times when you can get so fixated on one goal, and the harder you try the more distant it becomes, until you need to blink, and get a different focus.

Try visualising, suggested someone online. I would lie in the dark, open the throttle, climb out and turn over the quarry, behind the clubhouse, over the woods to the kink in the road and then line up with the runway as I cut the power to land. Did it help? Who knows. Besides, our Runway Two Six wasn't any old runway. I had to get to the stage where I could land at an unknown airfield and come down safely. Take the specifics of our runway and apply them everywhere.

The landing is the most critical part of flying, and at my airfield the circuit is over in five minutes. There are larger circuits where the same stuff happens in about ten or fifteen minutes, sometimes twenty. As you can imagine, that gives you a lot more time to take a deep breath and carry on. I remember once doing three landings, taking less than quarter of an hour and coming into the clubhouse to take a break. Ben said to me, 'What? You done?' 'My brain is fried,' I replied, 'I need a cup of tea.' At bigger airfields you almost have time to file your nails as you go around the circuit. The intensity in such a tight circuit is unimaginable, but once you have mastered that, all the rest should be easy. Or so I was told!

'Rinse and repeat,' my friend Edward would say. 'Life is full of menial tasks, where you just have to power through and get them done and move on. All that you can change is your attitude to it, but you keep repeating them.'

Recently I found the notes I had made at the time I was trying to go solo.

Goal/Vision	**Obstacles**	**Plan**
Going solo again	I mess up my approaches	Visualise how I get it right. 3 deep breaths Trust myself
	I worry about my abilities	Believe in what I know

Outcome	I feel unsure I can do it as a woman	Love myself Know I express divine love and power
I will feel confident I will be an inspiration to other women	I don't believe the men around me want me to succeed	Trust them and their positivity Trust yourself Ted wants to fly with me
I will prove something about women and older learners – they can still do it! I will make Ted happy	I fear it will make me stand out too much	Do it for all the women who can't manage!
Why I can do it		
I am a very good pilot I have worked hard and long		

Underneath I added things I would take immediate action on:
I will visualise landing and spend time grateful for my flying.
I will accept the process, however long it takes to get my licence.

Goodness! Dated two years and a month ago, there is that word 'grateful' again! Yesterday, I sat in a plane and had to pinch myself that I should be feeling grateful to be able to see the world from this vantage point. I had just told James that I thought I should give it all up. It's too darn hard for me! How easy it is to get so wrapped up in something that you forget how lucky you are to have it at all and how hard you have worked to come by that success.

8

Ground Handling

Trust the process

Going solo

'We'll do three circuits and then head out,' Ben said. 'I want them perfect.' 'Okay, that's fine, just remind me to take off the flaps when we leave, in case I forget.' I had no idea where we were heading, but I now knew better than to argue.

It was the morning after Farah's birthday supper, and I had been a little slow about getting ready, but the weather was perfect for a trip away from the confines of the circuit. I had been dreaming about this for some time now, desperate for some variety in my flying lessons. Feeling confident and in command, I taxied down the runway, stopping to go through the now very familiar safety checks. I had given Ben the radio headset, as he would be doing the radio for flying over Stansted, but I prompted him with the full call I would otherwise have been giving. The circuits were perfect, the landings a little less so. I knew how to climb, turn over the quarry, then again over the fields, looking across to the runway. I vaguely registered Dan was also in the circuit, but true to instruction, I left him to look after himself, worrying only that I stayed on top of my own flying.

Tom had been amazing to fly with, he had inspired me to feel I could do anything in the air, but only with him beside me. Ben, however, in his taciturn manner, had immediately handed over control. He had annoyed me with all those emergency practice landings he gave his students over the airfield, but if there was one thing that had liberated me more than any other, it was that. The feeling that if things went pear-shaped, I could turn this swift plane into a glider and get myself down in one piece. His gruff manner belied the fact that he had done more than Tom to make me feel I was the captain of my own plane. 'Don't ask me, you're the captain,' he always said. Now, even when I found it annoying, I knew how important it was. I was the one making the decisions; I was in command.

I came in to land on the runway I knew so well now. The plane thudded down and bounced, and before I'd had a chance to blink, I opened the throttle and was climbing out again, and then again. Both times I knew that the take-off was really escaping the fact that the landing was not perfect. The third time, as the plane slowed gently and then sighed onto the runway, I gave a whoop of delight. 'That was perfect!' I crowed. 'Wahoo!' We had taxied too far now to take off from where we were. 'Shall I backtrack, or go around?' I asked. 'Go around,' was the curt reply.

As we got near the clubhouse, I started to turn down the other side of the triangle. 'I am getting out here, and I want you to do a circuit on your own,' said Ben. 'Go around once at 500ft, just to catch your breath, then come in to land. You can go around as often as you need to. There is no rush, there is no-one else around. Just give me one perfect landing like the one you have just done. If you need me, you can call me on the radio,' he said, as he switched the headsets. I knew this moment was coming, could come today, if I was honest. Now that it was here, I was surprised at how calm I felt. It was just right. No need for any panic, any flapping. 'You are good, you're great. You are a pilot. You can do this,' I said out loud to myself as I stopped at the bottom of the third runway. I knew my voice sounded confident and strong, as I called: 'Golf India Alpha lining up on Two Six.'

It always was a sharp corner, and I'd often had to press hard on the rudder pedals as we rounded it, but this time there was no weight in the right-hand seat. My hand fumbled on the throttle, and I inadvertently opened it too much, realising with horror that the plane was now too close to the concrete path next to the runway. If I pressed the throttle as much as I needed to straighten myself out, I would be on the road. Damn! had I screwed up my solo before I'd even started, and that with my ground handling, not my flying? It was in a very different voice that I pressed the radio button and called: 'Ben. Ben, I think I need your help.' The timid tones would surely have them scurrying down to get me out of this jam. There was utter silence at the other end. Could they not hear me in the clubhouse? James was there, Ben, Ted. And no-one was talking to me.

There was nothing else to do. I was relieved there weren't other planes waiting to land, while I committed the ultimate sin of blocking the runway. I switched off the mags and got out of the plane, swung it round to face into the grass runway and then started up again. 'Take a deep breath, don't let that rattle you,' I calmed myself. Then I called again, in the same clear voice I had used earlier. 'This is Golf India Alpha lining up on Two Six.' I opened the throttle and took off.

Flying the plane didn't feel too different, even though both Ben and Tom had repeatedly warned me that without someone in the right-hand seat it would be much livelier. I took the engine revs down and turned into the climb. Over the quarry, level out. I was amazed at how calm I felt, how right this felt. It was just a natural progression. No butterflies, no panic, just the thing that had to happen. I was ready. Flying over the runway at a steady 500ft, I glanced around and was grateful once again that there was no one else in the circuit and the hoards that seemed to always descend at the weekends were for some unknown reason elsewhere. I came down to land, concentrating intently on crossing the threshold and rounding out as the plane bounced along uphill to a halt. Suddenly, it hit a bump and jumped, swerving to the left and this time I did find myself actually on the concrete of the path alongside the runway.

Noooo! It shouldn't have ended like this! I looked in horror at what had happened. Was Ben wrong, was I just not ready for going alone yet? I felt such a fool, having to call on the radio, 'Ben, I've come off the runway.' 'Stay where you are. I'm coming to get you. Is the engine off?' I switched off the engine and got out of the plane. There were grass tufts in all the wheel-caps. This wasn't the ending I had hoped for, I thought, laughing at the absurdity of it all. Perhaps Ben would let me try again and do better this time. I reached for my phone. Perhaps this wasn't what one would declare on Facebook, but it was funny, and I wanted a record of it. I didn't feel desperate or desolate, just totally ridiculous. Thank goodness there weren't more people here to witness my humiliation. I looked up to see Ben heading towards me in the club plane.

'Did you land it on the runway?' was his first question. 'Yes!' I felt a little indignant. 'I landed it fine, it just swerved to the left as I slowed down.' 'Well then, you did great. Congratulations. Could have had a bit more finesse, but you did it. You've done your first solo. No-one can take that away from you. Well done! Let's just check nothing is damaged,' he said as he pulled the tufts of grass loose. James was walking down the taxiway to see I was alright, and Fred was driving down in his beat-up car, but turned away when it appeared there was no harm done. 'It's fine, you hop in with her and let her taxi it back,' Ben said. 'No damage. Come and have a cup of tea, and I will take you up again in a little while.'

'You did it, well done!' beamed James. 'I wanted to ask if I can go again,' I said, rather confused. I had thought the landing would disqualify me. 'Don't be ridiculous,' James said later. 'Roy landed off the runway for his solo, twice. Actually, make that four times; he did it in the fixed-wing as well.' My phone binged. 'Well done!!!!' said a message from Tom. 'I told him it wasn't your most elegant landing, but then no-one's first solo ever is,' said Ben. 'You did it!' crowed Ted, as he leaned in to give me a kiss. I blinked. There I had thought it was all wrong, and now it appeared to be alright.

Going up later with Ben, he helped me bleed off my airspeed so that the plane came in much more gently. 'That's what happened there. You had too much airspeed still, and it hit a bump and veered off to the left,' he explained. 'There's no rush. Let it settle itself, don't push it down.'

'My ruse about flying over Stansted worked,' said Ben. 'Took your mind off everything, so you couldn't faff about the circuits. By the time you've done Stansted, there is nothing more to worry about,' he added. 'Tell James to take you off to Bury Hall Farm for a glass of bubbly to celebrate,' he suggested.

The photograph I posted online was of me and Ben. I was beaming with pride, and he was looking bored. I had done it; I'd gone up on my own. The sky truly was the limit now.

That's what I had thought that day, but it soon became apparent that Ben had other ideas. Whatever he said to console me on the day of my first solo, he wasn't about to let me go up alone again any time soon. The weather didn't play ball either, but every time I thought, 'Today!' Ben had other ideas. It was four weeks later before the stars aligned again.

Everyone is always so proud of their first solo, that magic moment when you go up in the air alone. Mine was a bit of a mess, if I'm honest. It got off to a bad start, and I am just proud that I still managed a good circuit. But the ground handling obviously left a lot to be desired.

The second one, however, now that was good. That was what the first one should have been. The circuits were good; the landings were excellent and smooth. I could even do a tight turn to backtrack in the plane and go off again. It hadn't look promising when we got there. James was checking under the cowling with the plane still in the hangar. The rain was lashing down. Ben was there with his cheeky redhead three-year-old daughter, and I thought, we've wasted our time coming here. Again. I had already had a wasted trip the previous week.

Ian was doing solo circuits as well. We ended up chasing each other, and I took that in my stride. 'Wait a bit because you are faster than him,' said Ben, as I sat on the runway after Ian had taken off. Once he was still on the runway and I would have been able to land but Ben pulled me clear. 'Can't land while he's there, he could backtrack or something.' He was getting me to do emergency procedures – took me for a dive above the clubhouse and I went towards Runway One Four, was too high, and he helped me turn onto Two Six in a one-wheel touchdown. 'Neat. Sometimes I surprise even myself,' he breathed happily. But each time I came in well; I kept my speeds constantly within the green arc and landed down the runway, sometimes a bit flat, but always safe.

No surprises when he said, 'Taxi to the end and you can go up on your own then.' 'What about Ian?' 'I'll tell him to wait.' I sat at the end, ready to turn onto Two Six, let Ian clear the runway, took some deep breaths and went. I wasn't scared or hyped. I handled the plane so neatly – coming very gingerly round that sharp corner. The hardest bit was staying above the runway. I had come down to around 350ft instead of 500, and I had to focus hard to get back to where I should be on the crosswind, not get too fast, and then go for the rhythm I know so well. I came in beautifully, touched down gently, whoopeed on the radio and turned to taxi in. 'That was beeeyootiful!' I hollered. 'Can I go again Ben?' 'No, come and have a cup of tea,' he said. He obviously wanted to check up on me and my state of mind.

It didn't take long, after a few photos, which James took, before he said, 'Okay, go up and do three more.' They were all lovely. They were everything the first solo wasn't. That moment when I was in tune with my aircraft and the air around it. Each one was a dream, kissing the ground, the landings were so smooth. I felt I could carry on all afternoon, but as my wheels touched the ground for the third time, Ben's voice came over the radio. 'I've got to head home now, so that's it for today!' A magic moment that I cherish, as others cherish their first solo.

It took another three weeks before I got into the air alone again, but eventually those solo sessions became more frequent, until the day I managed over two full hours to reach the seven hours target for the licence.

9

General Skills Test

Create markers to see your progress

The test

Perhaps Tom took pity on the fact that I wasn't getting along as quickly as I deserved with Ben. One day he took me out for a practice session for my General Skills Test (GST), the pilot's exam. He got me to do a 60° banked turn to the left. The gods must have been smiling on me right then. It was perfect. 'I couldn't have done that better myself,' he said. I had kept my horizon level, looked out of the window and held that attitude for a full 360°. The right-hand turn wasn't quite as perfect, but Tom obviously took another look at me as a student pilot. 'You will have your licence by Christmas,' he predicted. I wrote it down as a note next to that flight in the comments section. We went through the different manoeuvres needed for the test. Some are those you will use in flying constantly, others are the sort of technical thing you might have for a driving test and never need again. In flying, they are things like a sharp turn away from an oncoming aircraft, or a forced landing when your engine fails – and you hope you never need them again!

Instructors discuss students rather like a project. 'I reckon she needs another ten hours or so,' Tom told Ben. 'No, I think two or three more hours and she can take her test,' I was later told Ben had replied. A week later, Tom offered to go through my GST session with me once again. It was a miserable day for flying. 'They won't fly in this,' James insisted, 'it's far too stormy. You are mad to want to go up to the airfield.' 'No, Marco is taking a test today, and I need to be there and figure out if it gets cancelled on a day like today, or else I must be prepared to fly in this weather when I do my own test.'

I arrived at the airfield thinking it probably wasn't worth taking our plane out. No-one would fly in this weather. Not so – the student had been told the test was cancelled, but he had asked if he could do it anyway. Marco took off with him in the club plane, and as Tom and I got to the open area we could see them in the distance. They landed shortly after us. I was so pleased I had gone up in that wind. Now I knew I didn't have to be scared about the weather when I took my test.

Tom and Marco were chatting about a forthcoming trial flight day when there would be dozens of university students coming to the airfield. Afterwards Tom called me over. 'Now, if you can be flexible, I will arrange your GST with Marco. He's going to be away soon, so we'll try and get it done before he goes.' 'Oh, I am flexible!' I exclaimed and leaned over to touch my toes and show him. 'Very flexible.' The other guys laughed, but Tom wasn't amused. 'If you don't throw your toys out the cot, he may have time next week on Wednesday. But he has a lot of other things on, so I am not promising.'

I had been instructed to be there on the Monday to help with the avalanche of students. I was wearing a short skirt and didn't have my flying head on. Marco bounded up the stairs for his next passenger, and I told him I had made a sandwich for him. 'You can't bribe the examiner,' he replied. 'No, that's on Wednesday. Today you are just flying with students.' I paused. 'Aren't you?' I asked nervously. 'Nope, we will get that GST done, too. Now, who is coming up with me now?' he turned to the youngsters in the clubhouse.

My stomach knotted instantly. I went over to James. 'It's today! And I don't have my flying head on. I didn't prep last night.' I was panicking. Tom came past. 'Is it true? The GST today?' 'Yes,' he said with no remorse. 'I didn't want you fretting about it last night. You will be fine. You are ready.' I grabbed the manual and started paging through to refresh myself about the questions I could be asked. James and I went and looked at the propellor and the engine, talking about those tricky details Ben had kept tripping me up on when we had done dry runs. 'I'll go up with you first,' Tom promised, 'just to settle you down.' But it didn't happen.

'We'll go and have a fly,' said Marco. 'It is about finding out what you do know, not what you don't know. Just relax.' I got into the plane and all my training took over. My safety checks came out pat as I checked on him as a passenger. I lined up the plane and took off, sounding calm and clear on the radio as we left the circuit. It does help when the examiner is someone you know and like, who is out to make you as relaxed as possible. Soon we were out in the training zone, doing stalls, sharp turns and eventually practice forced landings. 'I told him you would mess up the first manoeuvre, but the next two would be fine,' Tom told me later, and I did just that.

There were some technical questions as we got back, and then, 'Well done, you have passed!' He would have rushed off, but I insisted on a photo with him in front of the plane. It now comes up as a memory on Facebook. I look at that happy face, and smile.

My flying blog

The little blue plastic wallet dropped through my letterbox. It was official. I had my licence now. I was a pilot! 'It's only the very first step to becoming a pilot,' someone said. So, what now?

In that last push to getting my licence I hadn't given it much thought. My journey from that first terrifying trial flight to my last cross-country had been a difficult and daunting one. Some of that was because I stuck out like a sore thumb at the airfield, but almost as much was because I struggled to find simple answers to the questions I was asking. Every bit of knowledge I have has been hard won, and much of it easily lost unless I hear it over and over again.

I looked around and realised that I was at a club that not only boasts the oldest active pilot in the UK, the charming Young Ted, but also had a wealth of experience of other members that I could tap into. I found what was written about flying very technical and obscure. I needed to talk to someone to understand things, but I knew I had the ability to then pass that on to others. Maybe I wouldn't be writing that soap opera with an interesting cast of characters, but I could help the next pilot struggling to make sense of what they needed to do.

That was the start of my flying blog, www.fun2fly.blog. It was my way of giving back, and a way of marrying my new-found skill with my creativity. 'The wonder of seeing the earth unfold beneath you got me hooked. Every day, every season, every light made the world look different,' I wrote. I wanted to share that wonder with others. Initially, if ever there was something I had to think about, it became the topic for a blogpost. I wrote about runways, flying in fog (don't!), radio practice, high and low pressure, visibility, seasonal changes, stretching your wings. Thankfully, Marco told me early on, 'Don't try to do more than you can manage.' I got Tom and Ben and Marco to check what I wrote before I published it.

No-one else at the club ever looked at it, but slowly I gathered some support. Soon I was chatting to pilots around the country, getting tips from them and making friends the way most pilots do – online. Sometimes we'd meet in person. I still get stopped at fly-ins by pilots with a name I recognise from my online conversations. Much of what I wrote was searingly honest about my struggles with confidence. Much to my surprise, the almost exclusively male audience found great accord with it. 'We're all terrified; we just don't ever say that to each other,' one friend admitted. So, it wasn't a girl thing after all; it's just that we're more willing to admit our emotions.

The writing has tailed off, as the novelty of each experience diminishes, be they crosswind joins or zone transits. However, I still have a growing group who love the photos I post online. My artist's eye was honed over years of watching my mother paint and seeing the subjects she found on her travels. Her painting was her way of giving back, of being witness to the wilderness she so loved and offering the images of an unspoilt world for others to enjoy. In the same way, my need to share is not about likes or followers, it is simply bearing testimony to a world of wonder that never looks the same, no matter how many times you see it. Just as Monet could paint haystacks or cathedrals endlessly because they look so different depending on the light and the season, I never tire of what I see from the plane. I know I am truly blessed to be able to experience that view of angels and, for me, sharing those images might help to light up someone else's path.

One year on from my GST

It was a year to the day since I had passed my GST, but Ben wasn't to know that as he hopped into the plane with me. We were going up to twiddle knobs and do the settings on my aeroplane's new radio. I did my checks and took off on Two One, straight into wind. We weren't 200ft up when he gave me an engine failure. 'Here we go,' I thought. 'Of course, this is going to be a long ride.' I pushed the nose down and said, 'I'd land right here.' Satisfied, he opened the throttle and we climbed away. The static on the radio was dreadful and I couldn't hear the incoming plane. 'I can fix that,' he said, 'just need to be on the ground to do it.' 'We can go back now,' I suggested hopefully, not sure I had the energy for what would be a lesson with him.

We crossed into clearer airspace and headed north. 'It's a long time since I went up with you,' I said. 'Forgotten it all, have we?' he asked. 'What would you do if we had an engine failure here?' as he cut the throttle. I kept my airspeed, showed him which field I was aiming for and came down quite nicely I thought, putting on flaps and turning final so I would get in neatly to the enormous field I had picked. 'So, what marks would you give yourself for that?' he asked as we climbed out. 'I think I did okay,' I countered. 'Didn't do the full Mayday call, but I would have got it in there just fine.' 'And what about if I had knocked the mags and you could have restarted it? Good choice of field, approach was fine, pity you would have landed short. You'd have come in on that line of trees, when you had a huge field to land in.'

'Okay, let's do a stall.' He sensed my brain-freeze. 'Remember how to do that?' As I was wracking my brains for the sequence of events, he was hammering me about not trotting through the Hasell checks, and although I did it right, I did need prompting. Thank goodness I had done a run through with Dan just a few days earlier. One after another they came – steep turns and every version of unusual attitudes until my head was spinning.

As we had left base, Dan had been heading to a private strip he had never landed at before. 'Let's go there too,' Ben said, even though we hadn't obtained the required permission to land (PPR). We overflew the runway, and I did a circuit, setting myself up for the landing, wondering why Ben was on his phone. Then I heard him talk to Kev, the airfield owner. 'Mind if we drop in then?' So, he did understand that Kev didn't like unannounced visitors. I flew over the hangar, feeling far too high for the runway. Ben got me to push the nose down and I landed, with half the runway left. 'You are always in too much of a hurry,' he remonstrated. Kev's first question was, 'Who did the landing?' 'I did!' 'Then it was okay. Just wanted to check it wasn't Ben, or I may not have said that!' I laughed. After a bit of chit-chat, we were off again. I was going to show Ben the strip I wanted to try landing on. As we left, another unusual attitude, but this time I was quicker on the uptake. I found the field and Ben gave me an emergency landing to get the aircraft down.

By now he was bored. It wasn't a teaching afternoon, after all. 'Let's go and play in the clouds.' I handed control to him, so I could take photos. We looked for a break in the clouds. Climbing up and heading back down later I sneaked in pics of the dashboard between images of the clouds drifting past us. 'I would have been worried the aeroplane would bust, at that rate of descent,' chuckled Dan when I showed him. The flight log showed zigzags and twirls, dips and dives, like a child's uncontrolled drawing. 'So, I wouldn't have passed my GST today then?' I checked with Ben as we taxied back to the apron. 'Nope!' he said cheerily.

I am relaxed and confident at the controls, and I feel like a pilot. It has taken the best part of a year. But I decided that Exercise 17C – the GST run-through – would be what kept me busy in the winter months when going places wasn't really an option. One must make certain one doesn't lose the skills, and that takes practice, practice, practice.

Cup of experience

'Make the most of the weather,' Dan had said when I passed my GST. I have watched him grow into a confident pilot in the years since his GST, constantly pushing himself to be better, but never losing sight of his guiding principle: 'It's a hobby. I do it for fun. When it stops being fun, I stop doing it.' On the days when I don't feel like going up, those words keep ringing in my ears. If you don't take the opportunities on offer, they may not be around for you when you are ready. Generally, the weather and the wind are constant variables. 'Go out and enjoy yourself when the weather is good,' says Dan, 'and you will build your confidence.' Ben frequently reminded both of us not to drain the cup of good luck until we had filled the cup of experience, an adage most pilots have heard. It is all about building a skillset that means you have more mental capacity to cope with the unexpected, which, in flying, is always to be expected.

It is sometimes not easy to see much progression in your own flying, so it is important to log things that once were tricky, and that you now find easy. I have never forgotten the horror of hearing we were expected to call 'Downwind' in a circuit I found exhausting to keep under control. Now, when I feel I am not moving forward, I remember that I make that radio call without thinking, and I know I have come a long way.

When you are new to flying, there are endless ways to stretch yourself. For some pilots it's all about ticking off the next airfield, but for me it has often been simply getting airborne. There's nothing wrong with giving yourself a pat on the back for getting up at all, and bonus points for making it all the way to the water tower. I realise after years of resisting it, I simply don't like flying alone. I prefer another pair of eyes and ears to make the journey a little safer, and a lot more companionable. Every winter or bad weather spell one's flying drops off – never more so than during the Covid lockdowns – and then you need to gently build up your flying confidence again. Even the times when you think you haven't progressed at all, when you are doing what is comfortable and familiar, something will be different, and you will increase your exposure to handling an aircraft as a pilot in command. Speeds, heights, banking angles, or just enjoying the achievement of being exactly where you are.

As a sensible woman, I would rather just keep flying than scare myself witless by going up when I shouldn't. Sometimes you do need a kick up the butt, but jumping off a metaphorical cliff face can simply see you retreat way back. I see it when coaching women out of their comfort zone. It's about nudging it, not blasting out of it. Not for me, anyway. Of course, you must push yourself, but only you know where your limits are right now.

10

Slow Speed Handling

Out of your comfort zone

Imposter Syndrome

I surprised even myself. We pulled up at the airfield on a gloriously sunny day. I looked at the planes that were out and the shutters that were up. There was no reason why we shouldn't be up in the air ourselves within half an hour. Yet all I wanted to do now was turn around and go home. I felt as much of an alien as I had in the early days. I just didn't fit in, and I didn't want to be there.

Flying is so much about your mood and your sense of optimism. Beware the person who goes up when they are down! This isn't a safe place to 'fake it till you make it'. 'It's a thing, mum,' Farah had said when I was moaning about not feeling like a proper pilot at all. 'It's even got a name. It's called Imposter Syndrome. And it's not something only women feel either.' And there I was thinking it was just a girl thing! I said something about it to two pilots who between them have around sixty years of flying, at least half of that as instructors. They looked at each other and nodded in unison. 'Yip, feel that all the time.' I gulped. It wasn't so special after all, apparently. It's just not something most guys are prepared to talk about, not at the airfield at least.

I often think of a little boy I know, who can tell you reams about planes, their propellers, their power – you name it. He's six years old, but you will find his grown-up version at any airfield you care to visit. There they sit trading names, like the rugby fans I used to know at university. Every game, every goal; they knew it all. But they only ever watched it on telly. It took me a while to realise, but it's the same in flying. The guys who talk loudest about planes they have known or flown, or sit and mock another's landing, are usually the ones whose licence has expired, or those who never actually got one.

And they simply didn't know how to cope with a woman in their company. I had nothing to talk to anyone about. I didn't know why I was there, or what I was hoping to achieve. Yes, it was fun, and I got a massive buzz out of it, but I felt as much confusion about things on the ground at the airfield as I did about being in the air.

I found out during James's training how preposterous my ideas around lesson times were. Now I was experiencing that myself. It drove me insane with frustration. 'It all depends', 'let's see', and my worst, 'suck it and see,' were phrases I learnt to loathe. Looking back in my logbook, it's only the flights that get noted; all the hours of sitting around soaking up the atmosphere don't feature. Admittedly, one picks up an awful lot around a clubhouse table, but it is rather like the ratio of screen time to television production time, an area with which I was much more familiar. It takes many hours to shoot even a minute of television, and then it may just land on the cutting floor. It's difficult to know when you will find a little nugget that may help.

I never felt a perfect fit for the role of pilot. I probably still don't. There are those out there who seem to take to it like a duck to water. The natural adventurers, the ones who embrace a challenge, who want to go on that terrifying ride at the funfair, and then do it one more time. I have never been like that, so it came as something of a surprise and a comfort to look around the airfield and see that the pilots there were very ordinary people, no-one with an incredible gung-ho attitude, nor with brilliant intellect or insight. Just your regular Joe, someone who loved flying and kept coming back for more.

I look back now at those early halcyon days, and they seem a dream. The fire and passion were coursing through my veins with this new love and the thrill of it. Absolutely everything was newly minted and undiscovered. It is an amazing time; but it doesn't last. Now it's more sedate. But the thing with flying is, it never just becomes boring. When the weather can change so significantly that one minute you are flying in admittedly not great conditions, and the next you are in dreadfully challenging ones, you know you can never relax.

But that's for the chapter on weather, not this one on Imposter Syndrome. I never quite stopped feeling it; not after my first solo, nor my GST, nor my licence, nor the Wings Award I earned. So, what did help that vague sense of unease, as if I was fooling others with a false identity? Well, every now and then, someone I truly admired would make a comment about me, and I would stop and think, Hmm, they think I'm good; why don't I?

Early on I had asked James, 'At what stage does it become second nature? That you just get in and go, like you do with driving a car?' 'Never,' was the short answer. 'It's always a big deal.' I now know that to be correct, and I have logged well over 300 hours in total. Every flight where you coped with a tricky landing, rode through some turbulence, handled some weather hiccup, or just felt in tune with your aircraft and totally in command, is worth fist pumping. You are always out of your comfort zone. The old adage, 'Rather be on the ground wishing you were up there, than up there wishing you were on the ground,' always holds true.

You're in control

Dan and I were sitting in the plane, watching the dance of the windsock. Headsets on, buckled in and warming the engine. 'What do you think?' I asked him. 'Dunno mate, it's up to you. Your call. At the end of the day, you're P1. You are the one who has to get us back here. If you don't like it, don't go.' I took another good hard look at the windsock. It was windy, to be sure, but gusty too. I was flying out later with my former instructor, Ben, giving him a lift to an airfield unknown to me, but renowned for its short, tricky runway. I had started the day feeling a little fragile, and what I didn't want right now was a thump to my confidence. I knew this was within my limits, but another day perhaps. I turned to Dan. 'I'll make you a cuppa then, shall I?'

No one was more astonished than me when I then got taken to task by Tom, berating me for not pushing myself to tackle the winds. The same guy who had told me, 'It's always a good idea not to fly, if you are not sure you're up to it.' Now he'd phoned me back in reply to my text. 'You have to push yourself! You should be flying now! You will never get anywhere if you don't.' He was still yelling at me when Ben sauntered over for our flight. I was more rattled than I should have been when I took off, but I managed to stay at the height Farnborough Radar dictated. Ben was doing the radio calls, and he showed me what was needed to get into this very tight airfield with a short runway, a pile of sand at one end and a row of trees at the other. The double-flap landing on a tight turn with a strong crosswind was more than I could manage. I took power off too suddenly and nearly landed us in a heap. It was a very dejected pilot who taxied off the runway. Ben's students hadn't turned up yet, and he killed time by doing a few more circuits with me, demonstrating how to balance pitch and power with what felt like a very different, difficult approach. It's not an airfield I will be flying into again any time soon, but by the end, I felt I had sort of got the hang of it.

I was surprised how slow everyone was to get their planes out, when they are so far away from it all that the instructor must fly in to attend to them, but it gave me a chance to chill. I was shocked by the fact that I could really have crashed the plane without Ben by my side, and feeling weepy, when I saw a text from Tom having yet another go at me about pushing my boundaries to be a better pilot. I was both incensed and perplexed. What did he gain from keeping on at me about my timidity?

Ben's student, a qualified pilot transitioning onto his new plane and bringing it back to our home airfield, suddenly gaily said, 'Nushin can fly home on her own and you fly back with me.' It didn't take me long to realise that would be a good stretch of my piloting skills. Without a passenger as ballast, my skittish plane is a different beast altogether, but right now, fuelled by my own desire to prove that I could fly, I knew I could handle that.

The wind had died down, and it was an exquisitely beautiful evening. The fields glinted in the late light, making me wish I could get a picture. Sensibly, I restrained myself, and concentrated instead on talking to North Weald radio and keeping a good lookout for any traffic. I flew towards our home airfield and saw with horror a tractor on the runway. But it was just Neil mowing the runways and he got out of the way as he saw me approach. I landed on that familiar Two Six with a calm sense of achievement, calling to the plane behind me that I had cleared the runway. I gave myself a mental high five for taking this challenge and, dare I say, flying with it. 'That was a spectacular take-off,' was Ben's praise as they came in. 'You shouldn't let yourself be upset by an argument before you fly, and you should never, ever allow yourself to be pressurised into a situation you aren't happy with. You are the pilot in command. You make the decisions. Well done!'

Just a girl thing?

I couldn't believe what I was hearing. The pilot next to me had run a flying school herself, had over a decade of flying GA, microlight and other aircraft and she was telling me she regularly thought about giving up. Funnily, that was exactly what I had said to James as we flew into this summer fly-in. 'Flying is just too difficult. I think I will give it up. It drains me emotionally.' I had stared out of the window, looking down on the straight lines of the Fens and their particular shade of green and brown fields, and wondered how much I would miss it. The tears had been streaming down my face as I mentally bid it farewell. I could still be a passenger, I consoled myself, I just wouldn't need to dig so deep to be P1 myself. Or put myself through all that inner turmoil of whether I could do this, or whether it was more than I could manage.

I blinked, now listening to Rachel. It could have been me talking, but she was light years ahead of me in experience, and, I would have thought, confidence. She was saying, 'I said to him, it's quite turbulent, it's going all over the place, I am just not feeling comfortable with the plane, I don't feel I am in control. You take over. I don't want to fly.' Was I hearing right? I had certainly never made James take over mid-flight. If we went up and I was P1, it stayed that way. 'Have you got kids?' Rachel asked. 'It's something to do with having kids. You become more anxious about life.'

She was telling me about flying with someone who wanted to be an instructor. 'Cover me, just act as if I have never flown before, I told him. He told me I flew well, but I know that. I am a good pilot. I fly better than most of the blokes that went to my school, but I am always seeing they went to France, to the Isle of Wight, to Scotland, everywhere. I don't.' I remembered the day I had met her in the clubhouse, a few months earlier, walking over to her and another experienced flexwing pilot, also a woman.

What were they talking about? Confidence. 'I just don't feel confident,' one was saying to the other. 'Doesn't matter how much I fly, I never lose that sense of insecurity about my flying. Why don't these blokes have it? None of them ever thinks, I wonder if I am up to that. They just get in and they go. Why can't I?'

Now she told me about how her instructor friend – the one who had to take over mid-flight – had sat her down over lunch and spoken sternly to her. 'What's the problem? You are a good pilot. You know that. The plane has had a recent service, nothing is going to go wrong with it. You have eaten and you slept fine, there's nothing wrong with you physically. The weather is great, it's not going to change and trip you up. There's no need to be so tense. You need to relax while you fly. The only thing that is holding you back is you. It's what is in your head that is the problem, nothing else. You can manage flying this plane back just fine, if only you would let yourself.' 'He made me sit up and think, 'He's right, and I can do this'. If anything, it was more turbulent on the return trip, but I relaxed my grip on the stick, just held it loosely. I didn't complain about the bumps, I just rode them. And I have never had such a perfect landing – I just brought it in so smoothly. It's quite a tricky circuit, but I nailed it. I felt so good about myself, I couldn't believe it. And since then, I haven't allowed myself to get all tense and wound up, and it's been great.'

'You flying back?' asked James with a twinkle in his eye. He couldn't have failed to see me huddled in conversation with the only other woman pilot there. 'Yes. Yes, I am,' I said. My flying time was almost twice his. There was a strong headwind, and I don't hit the speeds he does. It was a crosswind landing that had me holding my breath as we came down, but, hey, I held the stick back and got it down. 'What did I do wrong with that one?' I asked James. 'That was a bit hairy!' 'Your standards are far too high!' he exclaimed. 'Any one of the pilots at this airfield would have been proud of that landing, and you want to analyse what you did wrong. We are down. It was fine. Let's have a cuppa!'

He was right. Maybe it is a girl thing after all. We overthink everything.

Bits and bobs and boobs

I am now one of the regulars at the airfield. No-one remarks when I come and go. It's all very relaxed. I hadn't been around for some time, what with weather and work. My coaching was now taking more and more of my time, but when I walked into the pilots' hangout, I couldn't believe my eyes.

It stood out like a sore thumb. It was pink. Flesh-coloured, rather, with a bright pink nipple on it. Lying on the table amongst the dirty mugs, the half-eaten packets of biscuits, old magazines and engine parts. A very breast-like nipple, hard and erect, with darker colour around it. I averted my eyes, until I saw it there again the next time I was in the room later that week. No-one took the slightest notice of it. They were sitting chatting about the howling gale outside, the prospect of going camping, of holidays abroad and the plane that Professor G had recently bought. A low-wing GA plane with a constant speed propellor. There was something of a lecture going on about manifold pressure. It all washed over me as I wondered why on earth none of these delightful men thought that the presence of what must be classed as a sex toy could just possibly upset a female visitor. I investigated when the coast was clear, trying to establish if this was a computer mouse, and discovered it was a stress ball. You squeezed it and the nipple popped out even further. The thought of getting a stress ball in the shape of a guy's nuts did cross my mind, but these blokes would probably just laugh at the idea of having their balls crunched. You can't beat them at their own game, as I have discovered to my cost.

There were two other women in the room later, both instructors' partners. Neither of them commented or reacted. 'I would just have thought, 'How pathetic!' and thrown it away,' said another pilot's wife, when I asked if he was likely to find that at his airfield. My mate Dan shrugged and ruefully said, 'I don't often come inside here, and you know why.' Yes, he'd had pretty much the same experience as me – standing up to be counted just battered you to the chilly edges of persona non grata.

There was a time a few years earlier that I had done exactly what the pilot's wife suggested. Quietly removed the offending item. In this case, it was a poster that suddenly appeared on the walls of the clubhouse. A wonderful picture of a Spitfire, but getting out of the cockpit was a woman with the smiling face of Marilyn Monroe, hair dishevelled and in a sheer top that hardly covered her nipples. It was done in the style of the Fifties pop-up posters, with scantily clad women draped over fast machines, pouting provocatively.

I know one of the huge old warbirds at Duxford is a B17 Flying Fortress, Sally B, and above her name is a naked woman lying prone. It is owned by a woman, but it has a long history behind it, taking troops into the war, where perhaps that was the closest they got to a woman. Whatever. This poster wasn't a period piece, it was simply an excuse for a pervy pic of a woman looking like she'd just given someone a blowjob inside the impossibly restricted confines of a warplane. I wouldn't have minded a poster of Amelia Earhart getting out of a plane with her flying helmet, but this girl had certainly not been flying. I figured it was Bert who had put it up and moved it to the back room. I have seen him watching porn on his phone in the clubhouse, so he was the natural suspect.

That was the start of a new chapter in the war between me and Tom, who, I later found out, was given the poster by a woman pilot, although he would never tell me who she was. 'You should have asked before taking it down,' he always insisted. Perhaps, but the storm would have been the same.

Nothing was said that day, but the next time I was there the poster was up again. This time I did complain. I rallied support from the other male pilots, to say it wasn't appropriate. I got a very lukewarm response, almost all of them simply opting out rather than being counted. 'To be honest, you are talking to dinosaurs,' Simon, one of the younger men, explained. 'I wouldn't waste your energies getting upset. There are more important battles to wage.'

Really? Did he have any idea of how it feels to be a woman already struggling to feel like a proper pilot and have an image which explicitly reminded her, every time, that all a woman was good for in a plane was climbing out of it semi-naked, nipples erect. Dan and I still disagree about the poster. 'I think it was appropriate, and a period piece,' he insists, to this day. Tom kept showing me artworks of half-naked ladies that hang on the walls of major art galleries and asking, 'Why isn't this porn then? You call that art, but it's just the same.' Admittedly, I don't think I would want to see the Rokeby Venus on the club walls. I was told that all the club members thought it was ridiculous that I didn't want the picture, and they would have it up just to prove their point. I stopped complaining, figuring I had made my point.

One day the poster disappeared. Apparently, Suzie, a larger-than-life character who sometimes heaved into the clubhouse and told her tale of woes about the airfield she struggled to maintain, had liked it. Tom immediately offered it to her. 'Anything to get the bloody thing out of here!' 'Without backing down,' he might have added, but didn't. In its place is the beautiful WWII poem, *High Flight: 'Oh, I have slipped the surly bonds of earth...and touched the face of God.'* I don't know who put that one up, but it is much more inspirational. As is the ultimate truism which hangs on another wall: *'If you fall, I'll be there' – Ground.*

That stress ball, which my husband unceremoniously relegated to the bin, reminded me of those us and them days. The difference is now I agree with Simon and save myself the energy of getting upset. It doesn't surprise me, but it just reminds me there are times I am still an alien at the airfield, and probably always will be. The wonderful part is, I don't mind that. I don't need anyone's approval any more.

11

Unusual Attitudes

What are you telling yourself?

The impact of pressure

In fact, it was probably only a miscalculation of perhaps six inches, if that. That's the difference between a perfectly good landing and one that could write off you and your aeroplane. I was lucky to get away with a slight crick in the neck and a buckled nose-wheel. 'A mishap,' as a fellow pilot said, but for me, it meant I had crashed the plane. I was obviously no longer fit to call myself a pilot.

'You are the very last person on this airfield I would have imagined that would happen to,' Tom told me later. We had spent hours in the past few weeks landing on every runway in a variety of weather conditions. I had nailed them all. This was Two Six on a calm, clear day. There should have been no surprises. Yet I didn't only scrape over the threshold, I dragged it in with me. How on earth could that have happened?

'Make sure it is a learning experience,' warned Marco when I told him about it, with a catch in my voice that indicated I was doing a very girly thing and crying. 'Don't let it just be something you beat yourself up about. First you feel a fool, then you get mad, then you beat yourself up. Don't. Look at what happened, then pick yourself up, and learn from it.' He knew immediately which runway it had happened on. 'Two Six. There's a nasty little hump, just before the numbers, and even a gentle breeze can throw you about just when you aren't expecting it.' I looked up on my Skydemon trail. Seven minutes. That is all it took. I had gone up for a circuit with James, so that I felt confident of the conditions before I took Kian up for the first time. Now my beloved aircraft, my other baby, wasn't going to be flying at all, let alone take my son up.

There was a moment when there was a thud, and then the landing. I knew I was a little low, but I thought we would just squeak in. James had looked at the instruments in a way that yells disapproval to me, silently, and I tensed up. I added a bit of power, or maybe I thought I was in and took it off. Suddenly there was a thud as we smacked the ground. We were thrown into the air, but I don't remember that. I only remember holding back the stick as we thudded down again and skidded along the sodden runway. Kudos to me, at least I held on then and kept the stick back. I braked, terrified we weren't slowing down, and kept the back pressure on the stick. The first hump on the threshold may have caused the accident but, fortunately, the second verge on the side of the runway saved us from a broken propeller. The skid marks stretched down about a third of the runway and then veered to the left. The next moment we were teetering on the edge, and I wondered if the aeroplane would tip over. James said the engine had stalled by now, but I knew then, in that very long minute, that if we flipped forward, it would be very serious indeed.

We came to a halt in silent horror. I couldn't believe what had just happened. I was a strong, confident pilot, cautious and sensible. How could I just have come off the runway I knew so well, for no reason whatsoever? This had to be the end of my flying career.

There was no time to dwell on that, though. There were three other planes that could come in at any moment and we had to clear the runway. We were in an awkward spot here, blocking it for everyone. Where the hell was the CFI when you needed him? How were we going to get this beast back to the hangar? And where was Kian to help? James turned back and called on the radio, to tell them we had a problem and needed help to clear the runway. He took a look at the crumpled nose-wheel, while I held the tail down. We tugged at the plane as we tried to manoeuvre it. Uphill looked a long way, but going back down meant an even longer trek back. I wondered whether we could drag it across the crops.

One of the instructors had come down to help us, and we were figuring out a plan to drag and push the aircraft uphill and along the level runway. A visitor to the field told me gaily, 'It's nothing. You're not a pilot until you have bent one of these.' I looked at him with teary eyes. 'It won't cost much, just get this fixed, get someone to check it out, you don't seem to have done much damage at all. A few hundred quid, that's all. Only problem is, it may take you a month or so to get it in the air again.' I must have looked disbelieving because he quickly added, 'I am an aircraft engineer. I know what I'm talking about.'

I pushed and dragged until my arms were exhausted, holding my weight on top of the aircraft so the nose didn't smack down on the ground and doing an impossible shuffle along an endless track. Eventually Tom flew in, circled and then tracked up behind us, followed a little later by the flexwing instructor who chose a different runway. I could see James was flagging, too, and he still had to cope with the repairs, poor guy. Help came in the form of a trailer, and we managed to get the nose-wheel onto one side, and then had to trot along behind, holding it steady. When Kian appeared, I crumpled into sobs. Not only was he not getting a flight, but he would also now have to help his father fix this thing.

'We'll have you in the air in no time at all,' said a jovial Tom, who was in his element now. Brilliant under pressure, as Chief Flying Instructor, Tom came into his own in this sort of situation. People were dispatched and James instructed where to find a replacement nose-wheel. Kian and I weren't even allowed to disappear inside for a cuppa. 'Get the cowling off!' Tom instructed us. We sheepishly turned back to the hangar.

As the shock slowly settled in, I thought about what had happened in those seven minutes. It had started much, much earlier that day. I had been awake at 5am, thinking about a friend in a midlife crisis and how I could help her, when a loud bang, and then a second one, made me venture downstairs. Suddenly I heard breathing in the silence. There was another human being in our house. Adrenalin pumping, my breath came fast. I turned on the lights and called out, but there was no one there. For ages, neither James nor I could sleep.

I woke up late to a text from Tom asking for our ETA. James had been roped into flying a newcomer at our airfield back across the Thames to fetch his flexwing at Travers Landing. 'Noon,' I replied. I didn't want to add that James was still asleep from our disturbed night and would want to first check out the repair he'd done the day before. Tom was instantly annoyed. 'I will do it myself.' I didn't want to get James tensed up by telling him Tom was already in a foul mood, but now I had to hurry him up. Why had we agreed to help out anyway?

I was dancing between the demands of two grumpy men, trying to keep them both happy. As we left Kian surfaced, instantly irate we had taken on something else, when it was his day to fly with us. I didn't realise he was daunted by the prospect of driving to the airfield alone. 'I will come with you now,' he grunted. 'Best if you are independent of us,' I countered, trying to shepherd James out of the door and knowing how irritated Kian became at the hanging around that happened after flying. 'You will enjoy it more.'

Now it was three grumpy men, all of them mad at me. Looking back, it's no wonder I was tense. Add to that a lack of sleep and finding out, as we closed the door, that the thumping in the early hours had been a crowbar to our front door. I was soaking up everyone's tension. I ignored the sarcastic comments from Tom about there only being place for one pilot in command, as I tried to get Charles organised for the flight to Travers Landing. Blissfully unaware of any pressure, he only gathered his things once James had done his test flight. I was running around, making cups of tea, checking James had everything he needed and trying to ignore how mean Tom was being when we were doing him a favour. He made his disapproval very clear. Why on earth were we busting a gut to help things go smoothly for him?

Finally breathing a sigh of relief when the plane flew off, I was chatting to Dan when Kian called. He yelled at me for five minutes solid. 'I have cancelled plans for today. You guys invite me over, then change everything. There is always something else big on at the airfield when I am going. I don't want to drive up there and you are just wasting my time.' In true motherly fashion I tried to placate him. 'It's best if you are independent, and flying is just like that. Things change. We can't say no when asked to help with something for the club.' We tried to see if there were other days that would work better for him. 'I will come now.'

James called to say he was on his way back. Then Kian called again to say he couldn't find the car keys, and did I know where they were. It felt incredibly stressed. As James landed, I rushed to go up and get a feel of the conditions, so I had at least done a circuit with James before I flew with Kian. I felt under pressure to hurry so Kian didn't have to wait around. I wanted to be down before he got there, and I asked Dan to tell him we'd be back soon if he arrived before then. I understood how awful it was to go into a room full of old strangers when you were his age. I knew he'd be grumpy with us. That was colouring my delight at taking him up for the first time as a passenger. Why did this all have to happen today, I thought in dismay.

I took off in a rush, not doing my safety checks properly. I knew I was only ever going to do a longish circuit, but it wasn't surprising that Tom asked if everything was okay when I radioed a few minutes later that I was coming back in. His, 'Are you okay?' rattled me even further. On top of that, Dan was taking off and flying out. 'Answer him,' said James, and I felt flustered. I should have done what we are always taught – first fly the aircraft. Everything else follows. Instead, I had done what so many women do, I had tied myself in knots trying to please everyone. I thought I was too low, but that I'd just make it, and instead made a mistake that could have killed us. But it had started ten hours earlier.

The repairs didn't take a month; they didn't even take the afternoon. The next day I flew circuits with Ben, who told me in no uncertain terms that if I had just done what he taught me in the first place, there would have been no need for this. 'Land a quarter of the way in!' That day it was gusty, with a stiff wind. Round and round we went, until he made me land on Runway Zero Three. 'You see, you can land with a 15-knot crosswind, when it's gusting 24. Now go back and land on Two Six.' And I did.

Listen to your instinct

I was so thrilled to have passed my aircraft technical exam with a fantastic 88%, I crowed about it on social media. That was 18 months ago. At the time, one wit quipped 'I hope that 12% isn't what you are going to need to keep you in the air one day!' I was about to find out. It was my first away landing with a passenger, and I recalled his comment with a chill.

It was a gorgeous day, and I was taking Young Ted for tea at Old Warden. I had flown there twice with James talking me through the overhead join and circuit pattern, so I felt I knew the runway now.

I was lucky, because James had been signed off to fly from the right-hand seat. He's no instructor, but he certainly wasn't about to let our plane come to any harm – or me, for that matter! It meant I could stretch my wings with the voice of experience next to me, even though I was always pilot in command.

Ted and I had enjoyed half an hour and a cuppa in the sunshine. We'd chatted to some of the Shuttleworth volunteers and looked at the old warbirds. As we headed home, I had no idea that this would be the challenging bit of the trip, not the Old Warden overhead join and landing. We had cleared the wind turbines outside the circuit and were heading due south, when I thought I heard a different hum to the engine. I listened intently, then asked Ted, who has looked after hundreds of engines himself. 'Does it all sound right, Ted?' 'It sounds perfect,' he assured me. I frowned. I knew something was different. I didn't know what, but the music I usually heard through my headset had an extra hum to it. I checked the instruments, but the hum was getting more insistent now. Ted repeated his assurances, but although he may have spent his life listening to other engines, he didn't know the sound of mine. Something was definitely wrong. It was just a question of what.

It's quite a challenge being airborne, with all your senses on high alert and your mind in gear, trying to figure out what the problem you are dealing with is. What I was hearing was an exhaust nut working its way loose. 'They do that all the time,' the CFI scoffed later. 'Nothing to worry about.' Right now, I was another fifteen minutes from home, and trying to assess my best option. Ted could hear it too now. I had already figured out there was an issue with our exhaust, but what were the implications for an aircraft? In a car, you could carry on driving as long as you could stand the noise, but did the same hold true for an aircraft engine? Was I perhaps inflicting damage on the single biggest asset in our plane? I consulted Ted. 'Should we put it down in a field, or just push through to get it back home?' 'You keep going,' he insisted.

As chance would have it, a friend had had the welding on his new exhaust crack, and a section of it fall out of the sky somewhere over the motorway. He had made a precautionary landing at our airfield just a week or so earlier, so I had gone through his entire distress call drill with him.

On my first call to let our airfield know I was coming in, I was told there were two in the circuit, and they were using Runway Two Six. 'I have an engine problem,' I called, 'and I am coming straight in on Zero Three.' I wasn't going to muck about with a complicated circuit pattern and maybe find I had a bigger problem than we thought. On the next call I was told, 'The airfield is clear for you to land.' There are some plusses to having an issue with your plane. We touched down and taxied to the apron, the noise now so loud no one would have been in any doubt as to what the problem was.

Did I get any sympathy? Not a drop. 'Phah! It's a nut. Happens all the time. You obviously didn't remove the cowling to check before your flight.' Did I give myself a high five for keeping my cool and doing a greaser under stress? You bet I did. And I now check the exhaust bolts before I fly.

12

Handling the Weather

Grab opportunities when they come your way

A magical mist-ry tour – a cautionary tale

'November is the worst month for fog and mist,' said the Chief Flying Instructor. 'You wait and see!' I didn't have too long to wait before James and I were heading back to an airfield so shrouded in mist we had been advised to avoid the pylons on our normal route and come straight in over the village.

It wasn't lack of planning, or gung-ho flying. It was supposed to be the best flying day of the week. Minimal wind from the south, warm and overcast. A single trip had mushroomed into something of a club fly-out, and we were meeting a pilot from another airstrip too. The Skydemon route indicated under forty minutes there, over an hour return, so we knew we had a headwind. I had checked the weather the night before, and that morning, and the forecast was all clear. There would perhaps be some mist drifting in after 3pm, so we had to be back well before then.

Things didn't go quite according to plan. We had a blue sky overhead as we drove to the airfield, but the other pilot, Mark, said it wasn't yet flyable where he was. Fingers crossed, we agreed, let's see closer to our take-off time. I suggested that we get permission to land at Old Warden, too, just in case we decided not to fly as far, but it was sunny at Brookland, our destination airfield. Tom had texted from his lesson that the weather was good. He'd been halfway along our track up north, and the sky was clear.

The other two aeroplanes took off and we lined up. I looked south at a thick band of grey cloud and frowned. It had been gorgeous and sunny the day before. This didn't bode well. As we headed out, I looked back and wondered if we'd be flying home to mist and rain. It didn't look great weather to go anywhere in. 'I'm not happy,' I said to James. 'It's clearing,' he reassured me. I knew I didn't want to chicken out and spoil everyone else's day, so I just thanked my lucky stars he was P1. The others were checking on their position as we overtook them. 'You guys okay?' asked Dan on the radio. 'I think we should go back,' I said to James, just as the skies broke through with the promised clear blue. Perhaps I was being foolish after all. 'How about we do a precautionary landing at Old Warden and see how things look?' suggested Dan. We switched to their frequency.

Sitting outside in the sunshine at Old Warden, with a clear blue sky above us now, the pilots ordered lunch. I fretted about a text Tom had just sent saying, 'I would come back if I were you.' 'Hope you have your credit card handy,' quipped another pilot at our home airfield to Dan. 'We can't see the pylons here right now.' They are always our marker for visibility. I called Tom to find out what he thought we should do. 'Stay put and let's see if it improves,' he suggested. 'At worst, I can always drive up and fetch you.' 'It's the warmest time of the day,' said James, 'this should all clear.' 'But if it doesn't, we're losing light,' I argued. 'We have lots of options of airfields to land in along the way,' said Dan, 'why not go and see if we can get closer to home. It is clear here; we could always come back here.' It was only 12.30, and not easy to think of how impossible the weather might be in the little pocket around our airfield when the sun above us was beating down from a blue sky.

Mark had also had blue sky, but then it had clouded over where he was, up north. 'Think I'll bin it for today,' he said. 'Always another day, eh?' Indeed, very wise words. I knew I wanted to head back as soon as possible. By now, Stansted and Luton were both on instrumental rating, but Cambridge, the closest airport to Old Warden, was still visual flight rules (VFR). Surely, we could fly south and if we couldn't get home, we could always turn around and head north again. 'Just enjoy it,' Tom urged. 'It's what November is about, and it's an experience!' If I had answered him then, it would have been unprintable. It was definitely an experience, and one I'd prefer not to repeat any time soon. I was very relieved I was crew, not pilot, myself.

I had heard about sideways visibility, but never seen it. We took off and headed south over the wind turbines. Almost immediately it felt as if we had re-entered a sea of gloom and mist. James was flying lower than usual. My eyes were glued to the Skydemon track and the compass heading we were on, in case we lost the GPS signal. We were the fastest plane, and ahead of the others, but right now the prospect of turning around seemed crazy. We could find it had clagged up there and be on a collision course with the rest of our team. Pressing on seemed the best course of action.

The mist swirled past and around us, but always looking out of the side we could see the landmarks we knew quite clearly. The others were flying even lower than we were, and there was a point where the fog seemed thicker. I was about to ask James to drop down lower, but he'd already done so. It was an eerie experience, and an awfully long half hour. There wasn't even time to wish we'd never come out. There was only the sheer concentration of getting back safely. I looked at fields as we flew, assessing them for landing, but at no point did it feel that we were in any danger. Talk was minimal. We both were quite calm and getting back didn't seem impossible at all. Later, James said he'd never thought about what field we may land in, as all his mental capacity was focused on flying, and expending energy on an ever-changing target would have been a waste of time.

As we turned towards our airfield, visibility suddenly decreased significantly. We made our radio calls and James was going to track in along our regular path. 'I am sure we could cite poor visibility as a reason to go straight in,' I suggested, but he wanted to stick to the route he knew best. We got a relieved call from the airfield telling us to come straight in, and as the fields presented themselves at a lower height than we were used to, and I puzzled as to whether those were the barns where we turn or simply farms we don't normally register, I understood that both options had their advantages, the known and the more direct.

There were some anxious minutes as we waited for the others to land safely, before settling back into a clubhouse cuppa. We heard that other local flights had got caught out as well, and not been able to return to their home bases, and Ben told us he had looked up from his desk at Stansted when the weather had been clearing and suddenly found the fog had come in again. It seemed to be very localised, as pilots elsewhere were delighted by a glorious day's flying. The weather at our airfield didn't get better that day, but I was happy to go up later with the CFI and fly in those conditions, so that if I had to fly another time, I wouldn't panic.

What did I learn that day? Staying calm and keeping a clear head in challenging conditions are the most important things. You and your aircraft will land, but you can do a lot to ensure that it is safely. You are P1. It doesn't matter what anyone else says or thinks. When the aeroplane is aloft, it is you who must get it down. So, when in doubt, there is no doubt. Another time, I would have requested we turn back much sooner. There is massive peer pressure from other pilots, especially when you have arranged an outing. While I was hoping someone else would call it off, a new pilot later said to me, 'But you were the pathfinders, we were relying on you!' However much you study the weather forecast, accept they can – and do – get it wrong. Make sure there is always another day to fly.

Long haul – more than the sum of its parts

'We could fly closer over the coast. It might be more interesting.' We had just taken off from a holiday airfield in Devon where our aircraft had spent a week outside, and we were heading home. I was flying, and James was suggesting sightseeing. The answer was an emphatic 'no'. It took me a moment to figure out why. I wasn't even thinking that he take photos of the magnificent views I was seeing unfold beneath me – Cornworthy, Tuckenhay, Brixham, Exmouth. Village names that exist only in the English countryside. They simply didn't matter now. This wasn't one of the jaunts we had taken while we were on holiday. This was different. It was a journey. One with a destination on quite the other side of the country. And flying the breadth of England meant coping with vastly different weather patterns as we went.

A lot of planning had gone into choosing the right day for our departure. We had to be out by Monday, and, while we didn't want to cut short our stay, we also knew that the following week looked windy. Thursday was a lovely day, but we had planned to visit friends in Cornwall – a mini epic for me. That left Friday, Saturday or Sunday.

Leaving home, we had already found that what looks good on paper doesn't always translate into a great flying day. James had been packed and ready to leave when he learnt that Bristol was fogged in. The option was waiting another day or replanning his route. Flying solo to Devon, he'd opted for a route that didn't involve navigating the many military airfields the alternative offered. So he flew out the next day, and all was well. But what if you don't have a next day? That was the thought that preoccupied me.

Studying weather patterns on the Met Office charts, I thought it seemed that Friday would only clear early afternoon. Lengthy discussions with Tom, a whiz at meteorology, resulted in the decision we'd go on Saturday. 'It's the best day,' he said. True enough, Friday dawned misty and cleared but then Saturday started out with mist as well. I had a moment's panic. We didn't have that extra day. 'Never mind, you're flying into good weather, and the mist will clear before you leave,' assured Tom, sending a photo of clear blue skies to prove his point.

The plan was that I did the first leg, then we reassessed, although in my head I knew I wanted to do the whole trip if I possibly could. I had visited our first stop twice, so I had a better sense of the airfield than just from a map, and landing at home I knew I could do. James could do some flying from the right-hand seat if I flagged. 'This trip will catapult your flying onto a whole new level in ways you can't imagine,' Tom predicted.

There was no mist, but a fairly solid ceiling of cloud as we took off. Westonzoyland had assured us the skies there were clear. I was at the helm now, but I wanted to go the route James had flown, so at least one of us was on familiar terrain. Heading across the river Exe towards the red cliffs of the Jurassic coast I did request a few photos, but then the Blackdown Hills came up to meet me and I felt sandwiched between them and the cloud base. James became increasingly insistent that we would meet turbulence if we went higher. I was looking at what we'd meet if we went lower. We passed Exeter first, then

Dunkeswell loomed up on the left. I don't recall that part of the trip with the same pleasure as I'd experienced driving along its winding roads, catching glimpses of the spectacular views every now and then.

Suddenly we had passed over onto the Somerset levels and the aeroplane felt high again. There was a moment to catch my breath and then the airfield was in sight. On the ground, I realised how relieved I was we had broken the journey, even though we could have done it in one hop. Packed lunch, a cuppa and a chance to stretch our legs, and then I was doing my checks again. This stretch was totally unknown territory to me. I noticed the strange outcrop that is Glastonbury Tor, which we had once climbed and watched aeroplanes go by. The hills turned chalky white and undulating and I saw a horse etched in white. Further on, another horse. On the right there was a flicker of movement. The hillside was full of paragliders, swooping off the ridge. I tracked away to make sure we didn't meet them. By the time we got near Membury, which I know so well as a stopover on the London–Bristol run, I needed a break. I was happy to let James take control for a while; it felt like we'd never get home. Then suddenly we were back on known territory, and I recognised Reading, heading for a gap between two large buildings and noting the possible fields I could land in. The Thames came into view, a beautiful shimmering silver ribbon, which I knew from my Isle of Wight trip.

Back in London and its height restrictions, the last stretch seemed different and totally unfamiliar. I wasn't used to approaching from this angle and none of the landmarks seemed to register. As I navigated the last stretch and put the aircraft down on the runway I know so well, I recalled

Tom's words about keeping your head right until you are on the ground when you are flying home after a long trip.

As we landed on a sunny Saturday afternoon, the airfield was bustling, and no one noticed the returning heroes. Not even to offer them a cuppa. Nothing out of the ordinary then. I didn't know whether to be pleased or put out. Some part of me expected drum rolls and red carpets, but that's what pilots do, they fly places. And now I was truly one of them.

As a post-script, the following week had three days of high winds, one of them a named storm. I thought of the prospect of our poor little aeroplane tied down, alone on a Devon hillside, far from home. And I thanked our lucky stars we'd taken the weather window when we did.

13

Navigation

You are never ready – do it anyway

Plan, plan, plan

Where do you fly to? That's the first question most people ask when they hear you can fly. It's an important question, but certainly initially, *that* you fly is more important than *where* you fly. Just getting up in the air and safely back down again is what occupies most novice pilots. Only when you have that under the belt do you start to think about going somewhere, usually somewhere close and very well known. The transition from your home runway to an away one is huge, and the ability to navigate there without an instructor is one of the most basic requirements of your licence.

Most pilots will tell you with a sense of pride how they used to use a map to plot their flights. It's something you must still do for your navigation exam, although these days everyone uses GPS for their actual flying. Yes, you need to take a physical piece of paper with you in the plane, and I have sat with instructors checking off landmarks as we pass them. My friend, Young Ted, who has turned 101, uses only rivers, roads and railways as his tracking devices, and he does fine with them.

Like my son who uses Google to get around anywhere, but can climb mountains with a map and compass, it's important not to rely entirely on technology, so you can cope the day it fails. For my own part, I am delighted that my flying took wing in the Skydemon age. Despite the formidable name, Skydemon is a tracking system that gives you everything. It can plot a route in seconds, you can ask it about height restrictions, warnings, NOTAMs, different types of airspace, the radio frequency and landing fees at airfields. You can overlay it with Google Earth and see the physical space you will overfly. It makes planning so simple, it's difficult to believe anyone would hark back to the old days.

I'm a firm believer in Tom's sanity test. Basically, if the wind is blowing you this way and you want to get there, where should you aim? There is also an extremely complicated mathematical equation called the triangle of velocities, for which you need a large table, a navigation ruler, a protractor, paper and pen. That's fine for the planning stage, but when things change, as they so often do in terms of flying, you have neither the time nor the space for fiddling with equations. Sanity, now that's a word that always comes in handy, but the rest, not really.

Brian Woods spends hours teaching aspirant pilots the detail of plotting a route, choosing a diversion airfield in case you can't land at your chosen airfield. You look at the runways – all of them – in case the wind changes, and figure out how you will come in to land. What are the markers that will help you find the airfield from on high? Finding airfields from the air is an art that can easily elude the novice pilot, and even seasoned ones. They can be staring you in the face, as it were, and you still can't see them, so it helps to have looked on satellite views to register any features that may help you find them. I had a great big tarmac runway for one of my cross-country exams that it seemed would be impossible not to see from miles away, and I was almost there before it clicked into my vision.

My navigation exams, like much of my training, didn't follow the traditional course, so I was tracking from a less-familiar airfield, back to home ground and then back to where I had started. It helped me, though, to have the confidence boost of landing on a runway I knew very well, before heading back to a big wide one I found a lot more daunting than my own. It doesn't matter how much an instructor tells you than every runway is the same, and that if you can land on one you can land on any one, they all feel very different initially. Many of them have different joining instructions. For those who learnt on farm strips, the intricacies of avoiding pylons and local villages are less daunting than where to round out on a massive wide tarmac strip, and vice versa.

Before we left to go for a flight one day, Brian Woods was giving a navigational lesson to a new pilot. On our return, hours later, they were still working out triangles of velocity, and the day was wearing thin. When were they going to put all this into practice, I wondered. No amount of planning can consider how the weather will change, or what you will meet along the way.

Once, as I was planning a solo trip to Old Warden, Brian asked me 'At what height will you fly?' I looked at him in surprise. Old Warden is quite local for us, and as long as I keep below the London height restriction of 2,500ft, any height is good. The funny thing about Brian is that he never joins us on a club flyout when we go somewhere; he's always too busy working out the strength of the upper winds. I'd rather make a stab at it, make use of my Skydemon and learn the detail that only actually doing it can give you. 'Piss-poor planning means piss-poor execution' is the other refrain than often is bandied around the clubhouse – especially when something has gone wrong. It's a delicate balance figuring out just how much preparation you need.

Flying to France

Flying to France was just one such example – one that made me unpopular at the airfield, but one that I now look back on with a sense of achievement. I was over the moon to find a chance to flit across to France. After all, it could single-handedly qualify as the sole reason I learnt to fly. Little did I know the day would come when I was thankful that Tom called the whole thing off.

When I heard that a trip to France was in the air, I was determined to be part of it. Tom was happy to plan my flight to Le Touquet for the day after he went with Dan, much to Dan's annoyance. My instructor Ben decided he'd meet us on the other side with his daughter. He waltzed around the clubhouse scoffing at me fussing, while I tried to find out about the route, French air traffic controllers and how one logged a flight-plan. 'There is always drama with you,' Ben said. 'It's simple. You just press a button on Skydemon. And yes, of course you must speak French to them,' he teased.

In many ways, if he hadn't popped over that afternoon, Dan and I would have had a proper pre-flight briefing with Tom, and talked through the detail of what was needed, and maybe set up our timings. Dan managed okay on his crossing, although the visibility and the horizon-line on the Channel were very hazy. But then Dan is an extremely competent pilot, who doesn't fuss and panic like I do. On the day of my planned flight, Tom had a lesson early, so I arrived when I thought he'd be free to prepare. His texts showed he was clearly annoyed we were so late.

It seemed the stars were never aligned for that trip, and when the Skydemon account kicked me out as pilot in command for the second time because I wasn't the named account-holder, I started to worry. I was dressed in my crossing outfit, with the life jacket ready to be tied between the legs. The chilled and cheerful instructor was turning into a very irritated animal in front of me, and Ben's cheery texts about his imminent take-off at a nearby airfield didn't calm the mood. I felt a knot in my stomach. An annoyed instructor isn't pleasant to fly with and tension in the cockpit doesn't make for a good start to a trip that really is a big deal. Burly big Nick was delivering a running commentary on what was happening in the clubhouse, and Ted needed it repeated loudly to understand. I felt ready to cry.

I needed all of Tom's details to list him as co-pilot, and I didn't know his address. 'Didn't I tell you to file the flight plan last night?' he barked. 'No, you told me to leave it until this morning,' I countered. 'Well, if you hadn't been so late, we would have had this all done while my student was going solo. It needs to get submitted two hours before take-off, so the night before is best. But then you must leave at the time you said you would. You can't waltz in here whenever you feel like it. Haven't you heard the old adage, "If you've got time to spare, Go by air"?'

He was working himself into a fury, and I wondered whether I could pull out of this now. Fortunately, I didn't have to make that decision. 'This just isn't working, is it? It's not going to happen today. I think you should take off that life jacket and we go to the Isle of Wight instead.' I took off the life jacket with a sense of relief I would never have imagined possible. It was a hot day, and I was happy to put on my sundress again and hope that Sandown would prove more accessible than Le Touquet.

I learnt many things that day, the first being about allowing ample time for the logistics of a trip that requires paperwork. My friend Mark, who has done the trip as many times probably as the instructor, Ben, can do the crossing with a quick look at his weather apps, and a press of the button. For the rest of us landlubbers, it's a little more complicated. I certainly hadn't done sufficient prep for my Sandown trip, but I was relieved that I had spent a long time earlier planning for just such a trip that never happened. Tom knew the route like the back of his hand, but for me it was all new.

As we crossed the teeny bit of the Channel to get to the island, I looked to the side and thought two things. First, the best photo ops are always at times when you simply cannot hand over control, like right then, when I had to concentrate not to get too low but still descend, so I could join the circuit at the correct height. Secondly, I was happy that I only had a tiny patch of water to cross, as the line between sky and sea was invisible. Ben sent a photo of his Channel crossing later, which only confirmed how hazy the visibility had been. By the time I was buying Tom an ice-cream on the beach, the stress of the start of our day was forgotten. But not by me. The next time the possibility of a trip to France came up, I had the paperwork ready to go.

This time I was flying with Ben, while Tom was crossing with a syndicate friend. Ben never did stop teasing me about how easy it all was, and that I should stop panicking, but did I have my radio calls ready for the Channel crossing? 'I'll only take you if we fly in a straight line to Dover – right across Southend.' James and I went up so that I had the chance to speak to London Info, the countrywide frequency that takes you halfway across the Channel. Our radio wasn't working properly, so we wanted to test it out. I knew to keep saying, 'Student pilot, student pilot, say again!' when I couldn't make out what on earth they were saying, but the 20-minute experiment left me in floods of tears. Maybe everyone was right, and I was trying to do something that was way beyond me. I couldn't handle the flying and the radio. I sat and sobbed, wishing I had never taken up this blasted sport at all. 'How did you get on then?' asked Tom cheerily when we landed. He took one look at my tear-stained face and walked off as I said, 'I don't think I can do it.'

Ben calmed my fears when I texted him. 'I think we should cancel tomorrow. I just can't do it.' 'You just come along, and I'll do anything you don't feel like doing. And we'll have lunch in France.' Why wouldn't I go?

The forms were easier because I knew what to expect. I sorted the paperwork and I rewatched Dan's video of his Le Touquet approach. The day dawned bright and sunny and when we cleared the Southend zone, I could see Cap Griz Nez glistening on the horizon. This was 40km visibility, crystal clear. It made the crossing a breeze. The French sounded delightful as we switched over to them. 'India Alpha, we have your details! Bonjour!' I saw the landmarks from the video appear as I turned downwind and then came in to land. It was a magnificent feeling as the wheels touched that immense tarmac runway. I did it! I flew to France!

My French came in handy as we negotiated cabs and extra fuel. We were marking time as Tom and the other pilot touched down. A plate of moules frites in the town, a walk to the beach and an ice cream were unforgettable memories. Even when that cone meant my phone slipped and landed on the pavement, with a crack I was to remember as I lost a whole American trip's photos yet to be downloaded. Nothing could dim the excitement and sense of accomplishment.

And as we crossed the Channel again and I saw the white cliffs of Dover, knowing that I had managed to rattle all my airfield and home friendships in my dogged pursuit of realising this dream, I didn't care. When I handed over to Ben as Southend told us to cross the runway over the numbers, while an EasyJet flight took off below us, I figured I had done enough. It was only later, as I mused over the loss of those photos, and met the thunderous faces of friends, with spiteful queries about whether I was now too grand to fly to the water tower anymore, I wondered if I was right. Now that time has faded those harsh memories, though, it's only the clear outline of France on the horizon that remains.

So, Brian Woods is right about making adequate preparation, and doing everything you can to handle all possible eventualities. But you will never be totally ready. At some point, you need to take the step into the unknown and trust. Trust in yourself, in your wings and fly. See where it takes you.

14

Always Learning, Always Growing

Celebrate the wins, however small

Going it alone

'I will tell you. But then you must meet me at Old Warden. Alone.'
'Sure, I will drive.'
'No, fly. On your own.'
This wasn't an assignation. This was a challenge. One pilot to another.

Tough love. That's what friends are for, isn't it? My fellow flyer, Mark, was trying to encourage me to go solo again. I had done all my required hours alone in my aircraft. In fact, after that, on one perfect spring day, I had gone for a flight along Stansted's zone on my own. I have the awful selfie to prove it. (I know, I know – my sister has already told me off!)

After that, it was a matter of replacing an instructor I knew would keep me out of trouble, with a passenger I felt comfortable having beside me. Sharing an aircraft has meant that James and I built up many hours together. Initially I'd be the passenger while we flew into an unknown airfield, watching and learning the approach, and then I'd fly home. After a while, I would be the one flying into the new airfield, and James would fly us home. It meant I could build up my confidence and go further afield than I would have done if I had been the only pilot in command. For any given leg of a journey, though, there was always only one P1. No fuzzy lines of command allowed.

From there I progressed to flying with other pilots who couldn't fly my sporty aircraft. But what I never did was go up alone. 'That's crazy,' said Ben. 'If you aren't relying on someone else's help, then you could just as well be alone.' Well, no. Two pairs of eyes work better than one, and it is quite simply more companionable with a fellow traveller. Many of my friends thought nothing of it. They would fly with or without someone in the right-hand seat. Just as many pilots told me they never went up on their own. Why would they? I do remember once trying to school myself to jump in and fly alone. It was one of those perfect days, no one else around for company, but I simply couldn't.

The day of the challenge, I found a million excuses – all valid – for not flying alone. I hadn't slept very well, never a good start to flying. 'I'm not doing it,' I told a girlfriend. 'Another day,' she soothed me, 'you will know when it's right.' I didn't need to justify it to anyone else, because I hadn't told anyone of my plans. 'It's smooth as silk up there,' someone said as they landed. It did look good. If not now, then when? I didn't want to give myself a problem to solve. This had to be a challenge I aced. I took a deep breath and called Old Warden for PPR and texted Mark with my ETA as I checked out the aeroplane.

My memory of flying alone was how quickly the aircraft leapt into the air, like 'a homesick angel' Ben always said, and how different it felt without a passenger. There was so little wind, I took off straight from the apron onto Runway Two One and caught my breath as we soared up into the air. This was it; I was on my own – and it felt quite good. No wait, it felt fantastic! Like a muscle memory of an old exercise, I sat up straight, all my senses on high alert, and I smiled. 'I've got this! I know what I am doing. I can. I am fine. I am in control,' was what was running through my mind as I set course for the cluster of wind turbines that marks the entry into Old Warden's zone.

The half an hour sped by. I was enjoying the countryside in its yellow and green April splendour, looking at the patterns on the clouds, alone and loving it. I heard no one in the circuit as I switched frequencies, but a second call elicited 'Runway Zero Three in use'. Phew, with nothing to choose, that was the one I was most familiar with. Rehearsing my radio calls mentally, no one would have detected even the slightest trepidation as they came out. 'They sounded great,' Mark said later.

'Just square off your circuit, give yourself lots of room,' Dan had encouraged me. Now, even I was surprised at how perfectly my overhead join was panning out. 'Don't lose your height here!' I muttered to myself as I joined crosswind, with the same shouty voice the instructor had used at this point. I turned downwind just as Mark called overhead, 'in time to see your superb landing,' he later told me. 'Keep it flying, a bit more power, don't get too low until you are over the hedge, right, you are in, now look towards the end of the runway, pull back, gently does it, and you are down.' It could have been Ben or Tom or James or Dan in the early days, but it was only the replay in my head.

The radio is the last place for chit-chat at an airfield, but I couldn't help a delighted chuckle as I called, 'India Alpha vacated Zero Three, with a greaser of a landing!' There was no-one but Mark to hear, fortunately. I parked up and took the biggest smile ever in probably the only selfie that has worked!

I was on Cloud Nine as we sipped our juice, and I couldn't stop thanking Mark for giving me the boot I had needed to get up there alone again. He didn't really have anything to tell me, other than that I should fly alone more often. Will I? I am sure I will sometimes, now that I have broken the block I had about it. Admittedly, the trip home was a lot bumpier than going, and if I had met that turbulence on the way out, I could well have cried it all off. But I didn't, and that's all that counts.

Back on the stick!

'Pull back on the stick! Back on the stick!' I could hear his insistent voice over the roar of full throttle as this old bird trundled along the wide runway. So, I did. My right hand instinctively pulled towards me. The only problem was, I was finally having my first lesson in a PA22, a vintage Piper Colt, and the controls were the inverse of my now beloved Skyranger. Instead of lifting us into the air, I started to close the throttle – and abort take-off.

'Well, it keeps him on his toes,' laughed Dan, when I confessed in a whisper how the lesson had nearly come to a crashing halt before it even started. 'Keeps his engine failure on take-off skills sharp!' The instructor didn't think so. He opened the power and lifted us off the ground, while I sat in a muddled daze. 'What on earth did you do that for?' I just stared, wide-eyed. 'What words can I use so that doesn't happen again?' Well, yoke, for one. There is no stick in this vintage aircraft. A vivid red yoke on both sides, yes, and one of those push-pull throttles, plus a whole lot more I have never encountered before. Mixture, carb heat, a window-winder trim and a brake that looks like a bumblebee.

It is not often you get to recall the very first time doing anything, and my first flying lesson, where I sat in catatonic confusion, is happily now a distant memory. All I can remember is thinking, I don't understand anything. Why? What is happening? What is he doing that makes the aircraft fly? How does he know where to go? What is keeping us up here?

Nothing about flying commercially prepares you for the vulnerability of flight in a light aircraft. Just you, a wisp of metal and plastic, and the great sky around you. I think that first time, my brain seized. I cannot recall ever having been so perplexed, so far out of my comfort zone. It was beyond terror. The three-dimensional aspect of it also floored me. Remember, I wasn't someone who had been dreaming of flight since they were a kid. I had my feet firmly on the ground.

I know there are pilots who can hop from one aircraft to another, and well done to them. Me, I have bonded with my trusty steed, and I am in no hurry even to upgrade her. The Colt is a whole different ballgame – solid, slow, heavy, with all these strange controls, much less surround visibility, and yet moving faster through the air than my Skyranger ever will.

By now I can fly, I know what is happening around me, I just need to work out how to make that happen myself. But the lesson did leave me acutely aware of how long things take to process when they are new. It is like the time delay echoes one used to get on a long-distance call decades ago – you had to wait while the sound travelled down the wires. Similarly, the instructor would say something, and it filtered – slowly – through my layers of understanding and experience, before being processed into action. That all takes an extraordinary amount of time, certainly in a space where seconds can make a difference to whether you live or die.

As adults, we actually put ourselves in very few situations where we are taking new information on board. Children are soaking up new all the time, and that keeps them sharp and on the ball. Most adults don't go further than tweaking what they are familiar with. I know I had a massive recoil at learning a skill that was so far removed from anything I already knew. My instinct was to turn away from it. 'I don't do that!' is so much easier than the total confusion and overwhelm that brand new learnings bring.

Look at any older person you admire – what makes them stand out is their willingness to adapt and learn. It's not easy, especially if you are pulling back on the wrong stick! But it's a rewarding learning curve. Try it, you might surprise yourself!

New challenges

'Sometimes you just need a new challenge,' he smiled, when I asked him why he had started flying a different aeroplane. I didn't understand then, thinking I had all the challenge I would ever need in flying. Yet here I was, four years to the day since I first went up in the air with no thought of ever becoming a pilot myself, and I was waiting for the CAA to return a new endorsement of my licence. Soon, the way people believe microlights aren't quite 'proper' planes and their pilots the same, I would be a 'proper' pilot, able to fly a GA plane. Sometimes a goal sneaks up on you almost unawares, until you find yourself focused on getting something you hadn't ever thought about before. That's what happened to me with my SSEA rating – the one I needed to be able to fly a GA aircraft. It's why I ended up in Bournemouth, doing stalls at 3,000ft above the Solent in weather I would not normally have taken off in.

The Piper Colt, a green and red PA22 came into our lives almost by accident. We simply happened to be at the pub when Tom was forming a syndicate, and it was too good an offer to pass by. I didn't much like flying in it the first time I went up, finding the visibility so much more restricted than my Skyranger that I felt claustrophobic. Still, Tom had promised he would teach me to fly it, and I was happy to give it a go. I waited patiently for over a year, and still I had never been offered a flight. In the end,

I did what he hated, and started asking when my lesson was to happen. That probably sealed the outcome of the story, but it certainly was worth a try. We had had the plane for nearly two years now. None of the syndicate ever flew it, and Tom showed no inclination of fulfilling his early promise. Eventually I found Rodger, a retired instructor who was happy to train me in the Colt, seeing it as something of a challenge for himself to fly this unique old dame – the plane that is, not me!

I could hardly contain my excitement about my find, and at first Tom grunted approval. 'Do what you like,' he dismissed me. It was a no couched as a yes. I tried to figure out why. 'Now listen to me,' he then erupted, 'just go down to Bournemouth and get it done in three days. Then come back and learn to fly at your leisure.' My heart sank. James had done that two years ago, and his stories of flying made me realise that you needed to know your stuff before you got there. I had absolutely no knowledge of the intricacies of a GA plane. It sounded like the sort of pressured environment that would put me off flying for good.

'Clare did it, Ally did. They all went down there and got their conversion. You just pay the money, and you get your licence.' 'Well maybe they were better pilots than me, or you had spent time teaching them, but I don't want to put myself through that.' I knew I would rather do it at a slow and steady pace.

For a moment I managed to get his attention and we had two lessons. The one that sticks in my mind was on a November day that started out very rainy. By the time Tom arrived at North Weald, the clouds were looking seriously large and imposing, but it wasn't raining. 'Go on, it will be fun,' urged James. 'Up to you mate,' said Tom, probably hoping he could head home instead.

I didn't cover myself in glory, but I have a vivid memory of tracking towards an enormous cumulus cloud. There were blue skies all around, but these huge clouds dotted over the general flying area. This one had one half of a doorway shape cut out of it, as it towered miles above that. We tracked towards it, slowly and deliberately. My heart was in my mouth. I would definitely have turned away by now. This sort of cloud shook you around and could suck you in. 'You need to experience this,' Tom was saying. 'Keep steady, keep your eyes on the artificial horizon.' I would never have done this with James, but I recognise that you need to take advantage of safe spaces in which to experience a situation you may inadvertently land up in. It was like the slow motion of a movie. Were we watching disaster about to unfold? There was only silence, and an enveloping whiteness as we came closer. I held my breath, feeling the sudden shudder of the plane as we entered the cloud, then just as quickly we were beyond it, seeing only blue sky dotted with white. As we headed back to the airfield, Tom spied another small cloud, and I tracked right through that. Nothing can prepare you for how the cloud enfolds you, how disorientating it is. It lasted perhaps two seconds, but it was great preparation for later.

The next lesson was in the Skyranger, which meant Tom didn't have to take time off to go to North Weald. I won't easily forget the sense of dejection I had as I finally brought the plane to a halt. Who was I kidding? Tom was never an easy instructor to follow, especially when he was irritated, and I felt like I had done everything wrong. I couldn't trim the plane correctly, I struggled with my speed, I didn't keep the ball in the middle. There wasn't really anything I was doing properly, so how on earth had I managed to clock up over 250 hours if I was such a plonker?

'You are just wasting your money doing this in the Colt. Practise in your own plane. You need to learn to fly properly before you can fly a plane like the Colt.' I struggled to say thank you for my lesson. There were tears burning behind my eyes. It wasn't just that I had got into bad habits, it was that I had never been properly taught, I fumed silently.

A day or so later Tom told me, 'I got my students to change heights and level off, and they all do it properly with Attitude, Power, Trim. You just need to go back to basics if you want to fly a GA plane.' I spent days choked up with anger. Why hadn't I done those exercises with Ben, or Tom himself? How on earth could I have got this far if I was so bad? It made me determined not to have to fly with Tom again, and if I had toyed with the idea of getting that GA rating before, I was resolute about it now.

Fortunately, James was happy to learn to fly the Colt in the right-hand seat, and if Rodger wasn't allowed to fly with me, no such ruling existed for James. I started opting for flights in the Colt rather than the Skyranger and my confidence and understanding of it grew. It was an easy choice, as the road to the airfield was particularly bad that winter, and after having traversed the enormous puddles of mud, skidding and sliding, you then had the same on the muddy, rutted runways.

The strict formality of a GA airfield was difficult to cope with. There is no room for play with the circuit you fly, the height, the calls you make. It was all more relaxed and so much easier at our little grass strip. But thinking that wasn't going to get me qualified; it made me clench my jaw in determination. There was a time, only weeks before I took my test, when I landed with tears streaming down my face, convinced once again that I would never fly again.

I started lessons with Rodger, the new instructor. If I couldn't learn in the Colt, I would just have to pay. The difference between GA and microlight flying is enormous, and my sense of that hasn't gone away, despite being more familiar with both. In a little 'spamcan', your sense of being impervious to the outside world is stratospheric in comparison to the feeling of being incredibly vulnerable in the wisp-thin structure of a microlight, where you feel every gust. The GA aircraft seem so much more solid, and yet your overall visibility is so reduced. It makes me realise that we really do fly with our eyes on stalks in microlights.

The first time I got into the Cessna 152, I hadn't flown for over a month, so it was hard to decide what was just me feeling rusty, and what was a new aircraft. The lessons were spaced about a month apart, so I never got much momentum. Week after week, lessons were cancelled thanks to lashing storms, low cloud and high winds, but I did enjoy two sessions doing stalls in a corner of Southend's airspace. I know they say it's all the same to fly different aircraft, blah blah blah, but the little extras, like when you add carb heat, certainly make the whole experience trickier. Or they did for me. And on top of that, there's mixture rich or lean, wandering direction indicators, and so much more. I was just getting the hang of it, and my last lesson ended with me doing a take-off and a landing in the Cessna.

Winds of change

I had reckoned without the winds of change heading our way from China. Covid-19 was about to throw our known world into upheaval, an upheaval that would last an awfully long time. When my dear friend Ted shook his head and said, 'This virus will change the world as we know it,' I thought he was being rather over-dramatic. It seems not. Lockdown didn't seem possible in the West, but suddenly it was upon us.

As if she knew things were about to get worse, my mother finally breathed her last. I would often have cause to be grateful she wasn't there to wonder why our visits ceased, but she had taken her time taking her leave of this world. I was plunged into arranging a memorial service for her admirers when South Africa announced it was shutting its borders. Had it done so a day later, I could have ended up stuck there and unable to return for maybe six months. The changes weren't just about not flying. Everything in my world had changed. Suddenly, going back to South Africa again was perhaps something of the past. My fledgling coaching business spluttered to a halt as I contemplated where I was headed. I wasn't sure if it was a temporary diversion or whether I had altered course, but lockdown seemed like a great time to take stock of what was working and what wasn't.

It was as lockdown dragged on that I realised if I didn't do something drastic, I wouldn't get signed off this side of winter, and I booked that three-day intensive. We were actually pulling our Skyranger out for an engine health flight when the lifting of the lockdown ban on flying was announced, and after that I made every possible use of flying time. That included invaluable time in a friend's new aircraft and getting comfortable with a different style of throttle, airspeed and flying on a compass heading, instead of just bumbling along.

I had prepped every exam question possible and had brought the Colt in for a greaser of a landing at home when we checked in to Bournemouth Airport for my three-day experience. I had been so worried, I told no-one about my plans in case I couldn't stand the pressure and they came to nothing. Without all that preparation, I believe it would have been the ordeal I dreaded. The instructor Jerry was a relaxed fellow South African, which instantly boded well for me, and he knew just how to get the most out of me – calmly confident of my abilities.

We headed over to the aircraft in a rain-shower, which had cleared by the time I did my first walkaround of the PA28, a Warrior, getting to know the aircraft in even more detail than the Cessna. Three places to test the fuel, a long list to work through, learning to peer up the butt-end of the tailplane. My bête noire was the handbrake, which needed to be hauled up so decisively that I got a cramp and a bruise each time, and I struggled to reach down to change fuel tanks without being pulled back by the seatbelt.

We took off, heading across to the Isle of Wight. James was a surprise passenger. As we got up to leave, the instructor had offered, 'Do you want to backseat us?' so I knew I had Skydemon recording the flight in my bag, and a pilot in the back who would be able to remember things when I went into mental overload. I had never flown right around the Isle of Wight, despite landing there quite a few times, so it was fascinating seeing the other side. I tracked towards The Needles and then round the southern perimeter, in visibility where the horizon merged with the sea in washes of grey and pearly white. There were only a few stolen glimpses as I did my lookouts – sadly no time for photos. We tracked over the sea the whole time, doing full and partial turns, climbing and descending, slow flying and fast. Then we climbed up high and I got to do stalls all over again, turning time and again to face Selsey Bill or back to Portsmouth.

We were suspended in a gleaming patch of luminous skies, while to the side a huge cloud looked very threatening across the land. Dark and grey, it was backlit with shafts of vivid light hitting that watery coastline around Hayling Island. The Solent below was a shimmering, flat, calm blue. It was quite exquisite, and it took all my concentration not to reach for my camera but focus on how to catch the incipient stall without dropping any height at all. No one else was flying, except for one brave soul way below us we espied in the middle of a lookout turn. The skies were far too ominous for that.

I was pleased I didn't have to do the first landing, because by now I was cross-eyed with concentration. I was also happy to know that the instructor could get us back to home base on his instrument rating if needed – it certainly looked like rain across Bournemouth way. Leaving James to sit this out, we took off and did some circuits – some too high, too low or too fast. It was a lot to take in, but by the time Jerry suggested a tighter, bad-weather circuit to pick up our passenger – now waiting on the taxiway – I was getting it right. We headed straight for an unstable mass of black cloud. I thought of how dramatic it all looked and knew I would not be flying in this any time soon under my own steam, but I was happy to enjoy its beauty.

As we signed off from Sandown on the radio, they called that they were closing for the day. And then the strangest thing happened. That raincloud shifted away the closer I got, until we called for a re-join over a clear blue bay. By now I was managing the trim and the turns well, which made the next twenty minutes of waiting after 'Standby – do not enter controlled airspace, not above 2000ft,' much easier. Back and forth I flew at an exact height, keeping the ball in the centre as we tracked figure eights across the bay, listening to an extremely busy circuit.

'Bournemouth is even busier than Heathrow,' the examiner told me later, 'that's why we now do the radio, or our students suffer overload. There is never silence, even for a minute.' Part of that is due to the mix of aircraft, from GA to fast jets to international airliners. I was relieved when we got clearance to join the circuit. Having looked forward to making the most of the massively long runway and not land on the numbers for once, I got told to do just that, as we had a fast jet bearing down on us from behind and needed to expedite vacating the runway.

The next day my navigation exercise dissolved in cloud so dense the lesson turned into Instrument Appreciation instead. No hood was needed; I was concentrating desperately on the tiny window of the artificial horizon, trying to fly straight and level, and keep a balanced turn. I was grateful this wasn't the first time I had experienced cloud.

My prep for the exams stood me in good stead, and we whizzed through those. By the time I did my navigation exam and the GST I did feel like a proper pilot. I had broadened my flying experience in weather conditions that were challenging, to say the least. I had pushed my own boundaries way beyond their limits, and still felt in command of the situation. It was an exhilarating experience working with someone who felt he was there to enhance knowledge I already had, and it did my confidence the world of good.

There were no nasty surprises in the flying exam. Just two brief moments of respite when the examiner took control to peer down at an empty Glastonbury stage and at the furloughed cruise liners stuck out in Poole Bay (and I quickly grabbed a photo!). Getting a GA licence this way is not something I would recommend to anyone who wasn't up for the challenge, and well prepped themselves, but when I finally got that piece of paper in the mail, I knew I was a better pilot for it.

Epilogue

Run your own race

'You are a very accomplished pilot,' said the text. I smiled as I read it. I don't always feel that way. In fact, I often fight down Imposter Syndrome when I see other pilots heading up north to Scotland, or listen to their tales of flying across the high seas to Norway's North Cape. Simply following through on plans I've made for a day's flying can feel like a challenge.

I had spent the day before doing advanced manoeuvres over the airfield, sideslipping onto the runways, with what Tom called 'incredible accuracy.' I felt gratified by that, but most of all, I was proud that over the past two weeks I had gone up with my patient husband to practise forced landings. It took enormous discipline and lots of stern self-talk to cut the throttle. For the first time in a long while, I was feeling like those wings were still there. Sometimes it just doesn't matter what anyone else tells you, or even what you know to be true. What matters is how you feel inside.

The glorious spring of the early part of the pandemic galvanised my flying. I got my GA licence. James finished building our plane, and I learnt to fly it. We took every weather window we could to get airborne. I flew in the vintage Colt more than the Skyranger because its battery needed to be charged in flight. Every time I flew, I felt that surge of delight – back in my happy place.

As the lockdowns and restrictions carried on, however, and the winter extended endlessly, flying gradually became something I had once done. Instead of horizons growing ever wider, life itself seemed to shrink. The fear in the air everywhere dragged our spirits down. We huddled outside the clubhouse, talking to others at safe distances, often unable to land at other airfields. The joy slowly drained away.

I got my uplift from my coaching, feeling the thrill of a well-chosen question that helped a client think differently about her life and its possibilities. It was increasingly difficult to create the time and headspace needed to go flying, as I dedicated myself to getting another coaching qualification.

The time was still studded with memorable flights. Escapades like flying to Shoreham beach in the Skyranger and going back the next day in the Colt and taking a dip in the ocean both times. Tackling tricky airfields with Dan and returning in my own plane. Flying down to Devon to enjoy that stunning coastline again just before I did my coaching intensive training week.

Looking through my logbook, there's not much there that would tell the whole story; the shadow that drained the colour from all the joy for over a year. When Kian told us he had tested positive for Covid, it was an inconvenience. We were planning to fly up to visit friends in the Midlands. Instead, we hunkered down in isolation. 'Perhaps we should have Kian over here so we can cook for him while he gets better,' I suggested. Kian packed a small backpack. 'Have you got enough shoes?' I asked. 'It's only for a short while. I'll be fine.' He stayed for over a year. Every now and then, he'd feel better and try to return to his old life, only to be knocked back entirely.

Long Covid is a dreadful disease. I watched in horror as it debilitated my son and the active lifestyle he had worked so hard to regain over the years. Tensions rose as James and I struggled to understand its impact and tried to chivvy our son back to normal life. We would come back from the airfield at five o'clock in the afternoon to find him in his dressing gown, slouched on the couch. His plans for a 600-mile bike ride in the Outer Hebrides and a summer Alpine hike later were abandoned one after the other. Now he could hardly walk to the end of the street without a rest. Once again, I found myself between two grumpy men. I was drained.

Trips to the airfield were a welcome escape, a chance to forget the harsh reality at home. I never doubted Kian would recover, but as the months dragged on, his illness took an ever-greater toll on our lives. There was nothing I wouldn't do to help my adult son, but I wasn't always sure how to do so. I was a mother, and the son I loved was in need. I never doubted my choice to focus on him in this dark hour, but it wasn't easy. That uplift and spark that flying had given, was flickering. I looked back at the woman who had got her SSEA and wondered what had happened to her. I knew I couldn't finish my book on that high – life had got in the way. Suddenly I was back revalidating my licence, and two years had slipped by. This wasn't how I had planned things. I couldn't pretend I had carried on climbing into the big blue sky.

However, it was a time when I was profoundly grateful to others. Tom and I were friends again and he took me under his wing and helped me sharpen my skills. Dan would take me on incredible flying adventures where we landed at one field after another. A sympathetic comment from a stranger who flew a WWII plane at Old Warden gave me the heart to try again. Mark tried to entice me to France to visit the Louvre at Lens. Women who had started flying after me inspired me with their intrepid spirit. The community of women coaches gave me so much loving support I felt held aloft and able to embrace how my own life was unfolding with an even deeper understanding of the challenges my clients often faced.

Through it all, I had to find compassion for my own path. In flying, you steer around a bad weather patch if you can. As Kian began to heal and learn to manage his health and build his strength, James and I did too. The more compassion I gave myself, the more lift I had, the more I could look up to a bright horizon. I realised in life you can't always track the path you intended. Sometimes you take a detour. And that's okay, as long as you keep going. It's your path, no-one else's. The important thing is not to come to a grinding halt, because it takes so much to get moving out of inertia, as I was reminded every time I started the plane. So many of the lessons I had learnt with flying, and then again with coaching, came back for another reading. I had to accept what life was offering at that moment, rather than being transfixed by what was lost.

It was like the turbulence of summer flying that I spent so much time resisting. When you can go with the flow and learn to tolerate those bumps, flying is so much more pleasant. The silky-smooth flying of winter comes with its own drawbacks – lashing storms and low cloud. There's a shadow side to everything, and it's up to you which one you focus on.

It is the difference between being the architect of your own life, or getting mired in victimhood, where you no longer have any autonomy. Yes, you may need a period of wintering, of retreating inside to find your equilibrium before you can engage with the world around you again. We need to deliberately go out and choose the joy, perhaps at first only in the small things. The grand dreams may have shrunk, but while they are still there, they can grow and bloom again.

The past year had held milestones for both children, one getting married, the other getting on the property ladder. Farah's wedding was not simply a day of happiness when the sun shone, and flowers gave a colourful backdrop to joyful celebrations. In the months preceding it, I could enjoy the bond with my daughter as we talked and planned, and I helped her create this momentous event that would unite two families. They were precious moments, filled with wonderful creativity and bright colour. She did her grandmother proud, and it was a day none of us will forget. Just as the pizza eaten on my old plates in Kian's new flat, sitting on camping chairs around a large table – the single piece of furniture in an otherwise empty flat – was a significant occasion. It didn't matter that we couldn't light the candles I had brought because no one had a box of matches, or that the pizza was cold because we'd had to first unpack the furniture. We were all there and blessed to have the support that family brings.

These were the myriad facets of my life I had to rediscover to be able to embrace all of who I am. Everything I did was my own conscious choice, whether it was lugging furniture, helping choose a veil, watching a client untangle her heart's desire or deciding which runway to land on. Those wings were not just for me the pilot, but for all the woman I was. The more I loved my joyous, wild, messy, curious, creative self, the more I realised I could give myself all the uplift I ever needed. I just had to open my heart to see that view of angels everywhere around me.

Glossary of Flying Terms

Ailerons – attached to the wings, these hinged surfaces work in opposing pairs to help the aircraft bank and change direction.

Apron – the area between the clubhouse and hangars, which is used for the movement of aircraft before they enter the runway area. This is prohibited to all but pilots and passengers.

Ball (slipball) – an instrument indicating the aircraft is in co-ordinated flight when the ball is in the middle.

C42 Ikarus – a two-seater microlight, manufactured in Germany and widely used for flight training in the UK.

CFI – Chief Flying Instructor, the head of any flying school.

Circuit – the set pattern aircraft are required to fly to take off/land at an airfield.

Cowling – the removable covering of an aircraft's engine.

Cross-country – part of the pilot's examination; navigation exercises flying between two or more airfields a minimum distance apart.

Flaps – a device used to reduce the stall speed of an aircraft's wing, used to reduce the take-off distance and the landing distance.

Fly-in – an airfield hosting a gathering of pilots, generally by waiving the landing fee.

GA – General Aviation, aircraft that are over a certain weight limit. The section of the aviation industry that excludes both military and commercial passenger transport.

GST – General Skills Test, the exam a pilot needs to pass before getting a licence, which includes a practical flying test and verbal test. This happens alongside written examinations on subjects such as Air Law, Navigation, Meteorology, Human Endurance, Principles of Flight and Aircraft General.

Hasell checks – the checks for height, location and safety that a pilot conducts before practising any manoeuvres in flight.

Headwind – a wind opposite to the direction you are flying, which slows down your groundspeed.

Hobbs meter – records the number of hours an aircraft has flown.

IFR – Instrument Flight Rules, which mean the pilot relies solely on instruments to determine their flight path in weather conditions below those required for visual flight rules (VFR). Microlights are not permitted to fly in these conditions.

Mags (Magnetos) – produce the electrical power for the spark plugs.

Microlight – a two-seater aircraft where the total weight, including passengers, baggage and fuel must not exceed 600kg. The stall speed must not exceed 45 knots. Can be fixed wing (or 3-axis), similar in appearance to a conventional aeroplane, or flexwing, which consists of a parachute type wing with a tricycle undercarriage unit suspended underneath it.

Mixture – changes the ratio of fuel to air that is brought into the engine to optimize fuel combustion. Can be lean (with air) or rich (less air).

Nose-wheel – front wheel of an aircraft with three wheels.

NOTAM – Notice to Airmen or Notice to Aviation/ Air Missions – notice containing information concerning the establishment, condition or change in any aeronautical facility, service, procedure or hazard, the timely knowledge of which is essential to personnel concerned with flight operations.

Numbers – runways begin with the number of the compass direction, so landing on the numbers means you are landing right at the start of the runway.

Overhead join – the standard way of joining the circuit pattern at an airfield.

P1/PIC – pilot in command.

PPL – private pilot's licence.

PPR – prior permission required. Most small unlicenced airfields require anyone flying in to obtain permission beforehand to get briefed on the airfield status and correct arrival procedures, as many must cope with strict noise abatement limitations.

Prop/propeller – basically a wing with a twisted aerofoil section which spins around an axis perpendicular to the direction of motion of the aircraft and is driven by the engine. It gives the thrust to fly.

QFE – the pressure measured at the airfield, which determines height above ground at a specific point.

QNH – the atmospheric pressure at mean sea level, which results in the pilot being able to measure their altitude.

Runways – runways are named according to their orientation on the compass. The prevailing winds in the UK are East/West, so that is the most common direction at larger airfields. However, many small farm strips will create whatever runway their land allows. A westerly runway, at 270° on the compass, will be called Runway Two Seven, or an easterly one, at 90°, Zero Nine.

Rudder – the control connected to pedals used to move the aircraft side to side by moving the tailplane.

SSEA – Simple Single Engine Aircraft (a GA licence).

Skydemon – the most common UK GPS programme for private pilots.

Skyranger – Best Off Skyranger is a French-designed two-seater high-wing microlight, kit-built and very popular in the UK.

Sluka – a fixed-wing single-seat microlight manufactured by the Czech company Letov that is easy to fly.

Spamcan – dismissive term dating back to around the Fifties for a metal GA plane which doesn't handle well or fly fast but uses a lot of fuel. Originally, the nickname for the American P51 Mustang.

Stall – when the aircraft is flying too slowly to maintain its height and will fall out of the sky.

Stick – the control column for an aircraft, with direct connection to all the main control surfaces.

Tailwind – a wind in the same direction you are flying, which increases your groundspeed.

Throttle – the control that increases power to the aircraft's engine.

Trim – used to ease flying, it helps maintain a constant pressure on the various flight controls, often used to maintain a constant pitch.

VFR – Visual Flight Rules, which mean the pilot can see where they are flying, while using instruments to determine factors such as airspeed and altitude.

Yoke – one of the terms for the control column of a GA aircraft; it looks more like a steering wheel than a stick.

Zone – an aerodrome traffic zone (ATZ) is an airspace around an aerodrome, where all aircraft must get clearance from controllers to enter.

About the Author

Nushin Elahi's 20-year career in journalism and the arts in South Africa included working as a drama critic and an arts editor on two national newspapers. Moving to London with her husband and two children just over 20 years ago, she continued freelancing as an arts journalist, as well as working at the British Museum and Camden's Roundhouse Theatre. Her mother's art has always been part of her life and Nushin curated annual exhibitions for Alice Elahi for over 25 years, culminating in a touring retrospective and publishing a book about the artist.

Learning to fly was a sharp contrast to all this, but Nushin now has a National Private Pilot's Licence with Microlight and GA ratings. She soon discovered the lessons she learnt in the cockpit were those other women also needed, and now runs a successful coaching business between regular flights from her local airfields.

Fly with Me

Find out how to use these lessons in your own life at findyourwingsandfly.co.uk

Curious?

To learn more. Find out how you might shift things in your own life. See if those dead ends may obscure a path that leads to places you have never dreamed of.

I wrote this book for you. I wanted to tell you that you could do it differently. I remember vividly feeling that people could look straight through me, that I simply didn't matter, that I had wasted my life looking after everyone but myself. The sense of desolation that stretched ahead endlessly struck a chill into my heart. Does any of this resonate with you?

I remember sitting at a bus stop with tears streaming down my face as I finished a book which gave me my first glimpse of a different way, and promising myself that if I found it, I would help others to do the same.

I have done that. Watched my clients recognise the bars of the cage they've put up around themselves and see them evaporate as they learn to cherish themselves and rediscover the spark of joy in life. Many have stayed in exactly the same situation, whether at work or with their family, but changed their outlook and actions – and found their entire life reframed. Others have found something else that lights them up. None of them has taken up flying so far, although many have said they'd love to do so!

If you are interested in finding out more, download my free guide, *Find Your Wings and Fly – the Workbook,* which is filled with exercises and inspiration to help you figure out how you can also take wing. Life is an adventure when we open ourselves up to it, and I would be delighted to help someone else find even a glimmer of passion and excitement in their lives; to tackle life head-on, instead of hiding in the shadows. After all, we only get one chance at it.

My photography, one of the great joys of my flying, can be found on my social media platforms – come and connect!

For the workbook and social media links, visit my website: www.findyourwingsandfly.co.uk

Only you yourself have the power to change your life. But you do have that power. Embrace it.

I believe in you, even if you don't yet. I look forward to hearing the story of how you found your wings.

Nushin

Printed in Great Britain
by Amazon

18723902R00102